PROCLAMATION!

I HEREBY ASSERT:

I have the right to live in a peaceful world free from the threat of death by nuclear war.

YOUR ULTIMATE HUMAN RIGHT!

Since everyone in the world is threatened today by nuclear killing machines,

We the People

must quickly secure our ultimate human right that makes possible all of our other rights and goals.

> "Every gun that is made, every warship launched, every rocket fired, signifies in a final sense a theft from those who hunger and are not fed—those who are cold and not clothed. This world in arms is not spending money alone—it is spending the sweat of its laborers, the genius of its scientists, the hopes of its children." 1953
>
> "I like to believe that people in the long run are going to do more to promote peace than are governments. Indeed, I think that people want peace so much that one of these days governments had better get out of their way and let them have it." 1959
>
> Dwight D. Eisenhower, former
> President of the United States

*This book
explains the best
and perhaps the
only way to secure
your ultimate
human right
for you
and your family.*

You are not
helpless.

The situation
is not
hopeless.

It's up to you!

Meeting the Challenge

Since your future and the life of your family may depend on rapidly replacing the law of force with the force of law, we are making this book available on a non-profit basis. Please buy as many copies as you can and distribute them quickly. To help you do this:

- The list price of *PlanetHood* is $2.50. For only $3 postpaid, we will mail a copy of this book to any person in the world for whom you furnish the name and address.

- If you buy a case of 100, we will mail it anywhere in the United States at a cost of only 70¢ per book (a total of $70 postpaid in the U.S.).

- If you buy 1,000 or more, they will cost only 50¢ per book (a total of $500 including shipping in the U.S.).

Please order soon for our time on planet earth is limited if we keep on settling our international disputes lethally—instead of legally.

SEND ORDERS TO:
Ken Keyes College Bookroom
790 Commercial Avenue
Coos Bay, OR 97420
For Visa or MasterCard: (503) 267-4112

PlanetHood
The Key to _Your_ Survival and Prosperity

Benjamin B. Ferencz
Ken Keyes, Jr.

First Edition

Vision Books
700 Commercial Avenue
Coos Bay, OR 97420

PlanetHood
is not copyrighted.

Because our lives and all that we hold near and dear can be snuffed out by nuclear war, neither the author nor the publisher will make even one cent from this book. Any surplus above costs will be used to give away copies. We have rearranged our priorities to do our part in preventing the end of the great human adventure of life on this planet.

You are urged to buy copies and give them to your friends. Freely reproduce this book and use it in every way possible. It is our hope that translations in other languages will be made so that all people on earth can hear the good news: **a proven, workable way has been found to stop the senseless killing from recurrent wars that continually spill human blood throughout the globe!**

Library of Congress Cataloging-in-Publication Data

Ferencz, Benjamin B., 1920-
   PlanetHood : the key to your survival and prosperity.

   1. Nuclear disarmament. 2. Antinuclear movement. 3. Peace. I. Keyes, Ken. II. Title.
JX1974.7.F46 1988   327.1'74   88-70
ISBN 0-915972-14-X

Vision Books
700 Commercial Avenue
Coos Bay, OR 97420

*To Emery and
Wendy Reves
who have
profoundly contributed
to the cause of
world peace.*

CONTENTS

PREFACE

The Great News!
by Ken Keyes, Jr.

In 1982 I wrote a book entitled *The Hundredth Monkey*. Its purpose was to awaken us to the nuclear catastrophe threatening us today. There are now over one million copies in print worldwide; it has been published in Norwegian, Dutch, Swedish, Russian, German, Danish, Japanese, Spanish, and Esperanto. We all agree that today's nuclear killing technology threatens us. So what do we do about it?

I regard *PlanetHood* as the sequel to *The Hundredth Monkey*. *PlanetHood* describes the only way I know of that can be depended on to give our children a long-term future on planet Earth. It is not a utopian idea raising false hopes, or an untried scheme that depends on enough people suddenly being motivated by friendliness and goodwill—or fear and panic. It is based on realistic ways pioneered by the Founding Fathers of the United States in set-

> The very triumph of scientific annihilation has destroyed the possibility of war being a medium of practical settlement of international differences . . . . If you lose, you are annihilated. If you win, you stand only to lose. War contains the germs of double suicide . . . . Military alliances, balances of power, leagues of nations all in turn have failed . . . . We have our last chance. If we will not devise some greater and more equitable system, Armageddon will be at our door.
>
> Douglas MacArthur
> General U.S. Army

tling disputes *legally* rather than *lethally*. These basic techniques have successfully stood the test of time. And, as you will discover, many countries in the last forty years have been accelerating their development in this direction.

PlanetHood offers a *practical plan* for lasting peace and prosperity in the 21st Century. This breakthrough book explains eight effective steps you can begin taking immediately to bring a new dimension of abundance in your life and the lives of others. These steps will help you play your part in a *grassroots movement* that is now ready to gain momentum. Such a movement can enable the people of the world to free themselves from spending $1.5 million a minute on killing machines!

> *Our world family of several billion individuals on one little planet in the fathomless universe and eternal stream of time, that is the central challenge of tomorrow's Earth's government.*
>
> Robert Muller
> Former U.N. Assistant Secy.-Gen.
> Chancellor, University for Peace
> Author, *A Planet of Hope*

This is a do-it-yourself manual. Your future and well-being are too important to leave to anyone else. It's time to give up hoping others will do the job for you. And you will make your life count as one of the Founding Fathers—or Mothers—of a new world system that insures permanent peace and plenty on planet Earth.

INTRODUCTION

Why I Wrote This Book
by Benjamin B. Ferencz

All humanity has a right to live in peace and dignity—
regardless of race, religion, or political persuasion. A sketch of
my life shows how I came to this view and why I wrote this book.

TRANSYLVANIA TO "HELL'S KITCHEN"

I was born in a small and primitive farmhouse in a remote
village of the Carpathian mountains of Transylvania. Few
people even know where that is. For most, images of dark forests
and bloodthirsty monsters come to mind. Indeed, many legends
have been built on this foundation. Before World War I,
Transylvania was part of the Austro-Hungarian Empire. For
unknown reasons, my father bore the same name as the Em-
peror—Ferencz Jozsef (Franz Josef). Unfortunately, the similar-
ity began and ended right there. My family was noble only in
spirit. When Hungary gave up parts of Transylvania to Romania,
my family feared increased persecution of Jewish minorities and
decided to seek safety and fortune elsewhere. I was ten months
old when, in the cold of January 1921, we set sail for "The Golden
Land of Opportunity"—America.

We arrived in New York harbor penniless and were awak-
ened from our dream of plenty to the same harsh reality that faced
millions of immigrants. With no knowledge of the language or
special skills, life was not easy. My earliest memories surround
our small basement apartment in a Manhattan district—appro-
priately referred to as "Hell's Kitchen." Even in the worst of

times, though, there was never any doubt that America was an infinite improvement over any other place we knew.

I spent most of my early years in the New York public school system. Since I was too small to play most sports, I spent much of my free time in the library. I also remember going to the New York Society for Ethical Culture on Sundays to hear sermons that stressed the brotherhood of all people. Even at an early age, I felt a deep yearning for universal friendship and world peace.

I was enrolled in a special high school with an accelerated curriculum. My training there qualified me for an academic scholarship to the New York City College. It was a proud day for my family when four years later I acquired a degree in social sciences.

My only ambition during those early years was to become a lawyer. I considered myself fortunate, therefore, to be admitted to Harvard Law School. I managed to win a scholarship and earned my keep by waiting on tables, tutoring, and doing research for one of my professors, a leading criminologist writing a book on war crimes.

> *MAKE US EFFECTIVE AND USEFUL FOR THE ADVANCEMENT OF THE CAUSE OF PEACE AND JUSTICE AND LIBERTY IN THE WORLD.*
> Inscription over a portal at the Harvard Law School Library

Through him I acquired an expertise which was to have a profound influence on my later life.

NORMANDY BEACH TO DACHAU

The United States army had little use for lawyers when America entered World War II. After I graduated from Harvard in 1943, I joined an antiaircraft artillery battalion preparing for the invasion of France. I was to return to my native continent, though not under the best of circumstances. I plunged into the sea at "Omaha Beach" in Normandy and was baptized by the tide of a world at war. As an enlisted man in the army under General Patton, I fought in every campaign in Europe.

Despite the perils and hardships, I did not fully grasp the horrors of war until we began to uncover evidence of Nazi atrocities. I was soon transferred to a newly created War Crimes Branch of the Army to gather evidence of Nazi brutality and apprehend the criminals. It was only then that my unique knowledge of war crimes law was at last put to use.

It was a grisly assignment. Among my duties, I had to dig up bodies of young American flyers who had parachuted or crashed, and were beaten to death by enraged German mobs or murdered by local Gestapo officials. This, however, was merely the initiation to horrors yet to come. It was not until I joined the American troops advancing toward German concentration camps that I realized the full extent of the Nazi terror.

Indelibly seared into my memory are the scenes I witnessed while liberating these centers of death and destruction. Camps like Buchenwald, Mauthausen, and Dachau are vividly imprinted in my mind's eye. Even today, when I close my eyes, I witness a deadly vision I can never forget—the crematoria aglow with the fire of burning flesh, the mounds of emaciated corpses stacked like cordwood waiting to be burned. *Most of all, though, I will never forget the stench of rotting or burning bodies.*

It was often impossible to tell whether the skeleton-like inmates lying near-naked in the dust were dead or alive. Those who could walk had been whisked away by panic-stricken SS guards. Their flight

> *The dream of a world united against the awful wastes of war is ... deeply imbedded in the hearts of men everywhere.*
> Woodrow Wilson
> Former U.S. President
> When advocating the League of Nations

was made visible only by the trail of dead bodies strewn along the road. The bedraggled prisoners who could not keep pace with the retreat were shot on the spot and left dead or dying. I helped to uncover many mass graves where innocent victims had been massacred.

I had peered into Hell. *I had seen the brutalizing effects of man's inhumanity to man.* As I went about my grim duties, I was filled with a silent numbness. It was as if my mind had built an emotional wall to avoid going mad. There were no tears or wild cries for vengeance. *But the days of my laughing boyhood were over.*

HISTORY'S BIGGEST MURDER TRIAL

On the day after Christmas 1945, I was honorably discharged from the U.S. Army with the rank of Sergeant of Infantry. I returned to New York and prepared to practice law. Shortly thereafter, I received a telegram inviting me to come to the Pentagon in Washington. There I met Colonel "Mickey" Marcus, a flamboyant West Pointer who had been a District Attorney in New York. He was recruiting lawyers for the Nuremberg war crimes trials.

> *Let us be . . . cherishing our cultural and folkloric diversity, but not letting these differences become the source and instruments of hatred, divisions and wars.*
>
> Robert Muller
> Former U.N. Assistant Secy.-Gen.
> *What War Taught Me About Peace*

The trial against Goering and other Nazi leaders was already in progress. He urged me to go back to Germany as a civilian prosecutor for the United States offering me the simulated rank of Colonel. I joined the staff of Colonel (later General) Telford Taylor, a Harvard Law man with a distinguished legal background. The U.S. had decided to prosecute a broad cross section of Nazi criminals once the trial against Goering and his henchmen was over. Taylor was to be the Chief of Counsel for a dozen subsequent Nuremberg trials which had to be prepared in a hurry.

Taylor sent me with about fifty researchers to Berlin to scour Nazi offices and archives. No one could be indicted without evidence of personal guilt beyond any reasonable doubt. The records we uncovered were to form the basis for trials against German doctors, lawyers, judges, generals, industrialists, and others who played leading roles in organizing or perpetrating Nazi brutalities.

One day, one of our investigators was stunned by the discovery of a number of files uncovered in the cellar of the burned-out Gestapo headquarters. They were top secret reports chronicling the number of people slaughtered by special SS extermination squads called *Einsatzgruppen*. Their crimes were horrendous. Without pity or remorse, the SS murder squads killed every Jewish man, woman, and child they could lay their hands on. Gypsies, communist functionaries, and Soviet intellectuals suffered the same fate. *I tabulated over a million persons deliberately murdered by these special "action groups."* The disclosure of unmitigated cruelty screamed out for justice. I flew to Nuremberg with the evidence and presented it to General Taylor who bore the final responsibility for the prosecutions.

In our hands lay overwhelming evidence of Nazi genocide. The General immediately recognized the vast importance and impact these documents would have. We vowed not to allow these mass murderers to escape trial. The case was assigned to me. I became Chief Prosecutor for the United States in what the Associated Press called "the biggest murder trial in history."

Twenty-two defendants were charged with murdering over a million people. I was only twenty-seven years old. It was my first case.

> *The defendants in the dock were the cruel executioners, whose terror wrote the blackest page in human history. Death was their tool and life was their toy. If these men be immune, then law has lost its meaning and man must live in fear.*
>
> Benjamin B. Ferencz
> Opening Statement, Einsatzgruppen Trial
> Nuremberg, 1947

What sentence could I possibly ask the court to impose for such crimes? How does one draw a balance between the lives of twenty-two guilty Germans and their horrendous crimes against humanity? It seemed that hanging the lot was not enough. The significance of these proceedings should have an impact on the future. The entire human race had to be protected from the lawlessness of tyrants.

"May it please your Honors," I said as I addressed the tribunal, "It is with sorrow and with hope that we here disclose the

18

deliberate slaughter of more than a million innocent and defense-less men, women, and children. This was the tragic fulfillment of a program of intolerance and arrogance. Vengeance is not our goal, nor do we seek merely a just retribution. *We ask this Court to affirm by international penal action man's right to live in peace and dignity regardless of his race or creed. The case we present is a plea of humanity to law."*

After the trial which lasted a year and a half, all of the defen-dants were convicted. Thirteen were sentenced to death. The verdict was hailed as a great success for the prosecution. My pri-mary objective had been to establish *a legal precedent that would encourage a more humane and secure world in the future.*

Though many of the Nazi atrocities were carried out by nothing less than sadists or professional criminals, those who conceived and directed the extermination programs were quite different. I was shocked to learn that almost all of them were educated men who seemed quite normal. They loved their fami-lies, were kind to cats and dogs, enjoyed Wagner's music, and could quote Goethe's poetry. In fact, many of them—I am ashamed to say—were lawyers.

Even today, as I look back upon this dark chapter in human history, I am dumbfounded by the complete lack of remorse with which these white-collar mass murderers seemed to operate. Regret was practically nonexistent while de-nial of the truth, self-pity, and false accusa-tions against others were commonplace. I soon realized that if one begins with the distorted conviction that a person of a certain race, opinion, or belief is inferior, his extermination seems logical and even desirable.

> *However intense may be a group's moral conviction of the rightness of its particular religion or ideology, it should in its own interest function within the univer-sally accepted system of law and politics aimed at order and justice.*
>
> Quincy Wright, 1962
> Professor of International Law
> University of Chicago

Nuremberg taught me that creating a world of tolerance and compassion would be a long and arduous task. And I also learned that if we did not devote ourselves to developing effective world law, the same cruel mentality that made the Holocaust possible might one day destroy the entire human race.

COMPENSATING HITLER'S VICTIMS

There are many steps in this process we call justice—punishing the guilty is only one. Rehabilitating the victims is a longer and perhaps more important task. After the war crimes trials were over, I remained in Germany to recover assets stolen from those who had been murdered. The proceeds were to benefit the survivors of Nazi persecution. A network of offices was

> *We appeal as human beings to human beings: Remember your humanity, and forget the rest.*
>
> Albert Einstein
> Last public statement, 1955

organized throughout the world to help them with their claims and compensation. I participated in negotiations which resulted in new German laws benefiting these victims.

My aim was to seek justice under law and to make life more tolerable for those who had been carried out of the concentration camps with only their crippling wounds and bitter memories. Working with survivors increased my determination to do whatever I could to prevent such great tragedies from ever happening again.

I returned to New York in 1956 and joined in a law partnership with my former chief, Telford Taylor. In addition to being colleagues at Nuremberg, we had another rather special bond. One rainy afternoon in 1948, we had faced death together. We and our wives had been forced to parachute out of a falling plane over the ruins in Berlin. We were "survivors" in our own way, which I believe gave me an increased sympathy for those who had survived the horror of Hitler's persecutions.

The war had ended, some Nazi criminals had been brought to justice, but the indelible mark of violence, left deep within the soul of millions of innocents, lingered on. Jewish organizations offered modest retainers for me to continue to act for them on restitution problems. I also represented churches of many denominations which had lost foreign missionary properties during the war. What I found most satisfying, though, was the opportunity to advance international law and to promote the human rights of needy persons or those who had been deprived of justice.

AIDING HUMAN "GUINEA PIGS"

A plan to help Catholic Polish women who had been victims of Nazi medical experiments was broached by a devout and kindly lady from New York. Caroline Ferriday first took the idea to Norman Cousins, then editor of the highly-esteemed magazine *Saturday Review of Literature* and today President of the World Federalist Association and one of America's most avid and articulate campaigners for World Federal Government.

Cousins had arranged in 1955 to bring some young Japanese women from Hiroshima to the United States. They had been disfigured when the U.S. dropped the first atomic bomb. American plastic surgeons helped to remove some of their physical scars. This humanitarian assistance to the "Hiroshima Maidens" was widely appreciated as a gesture of reconciliation and remorse. Miss Ferriday asked Cousins to do something similar for Polish women who, as inmates of the Ravensbrueck concentration camp, had been used as human guinea pigs by German doctors. Cousins promised to try.

> We have grasped the mystery of the atom and rejected the Sermon on the Mount. Ours is a world of nuclear giants and ethical infants. We know more about killing than we do about living.
>
> Omar Bradley
> General, U.S. Army

A small committee was formed and I was invited to serve as legal counsel. I directed my efforts at trying to obtain compensation from the German government. It had no diplomatic relations with Poland, and Polish nationals were not eligible under

Germany's indemnification laws. With great difficulty, the German cabinet was finally persuaded to make an exception. The payments by the Federal Republic made an enormous difference in the lives of those surprised women in Poland.

Those who had been forced to work as slaves for Hitler also became surprised beneficiaries of payments squeezed out of some leading German firms. The full story is told in my book *Less Than Slaves*, published by Harvard University Press. I concluded that the deliberate attempt to "work people to death" was made possible only by human indifference to suffering. The German edition was made into a TV documentary which had a significant impact on the new German generation. I was glad to see that some of them had the courage to speak out for a more humane society.

THE PEN VERSUS THE SWORD

In 1970, with the United States sinking ever deeper into the quagmire of Vietnam, it was only natural that my mind should turn to the *need for a peaceful world.* Over fifty thousand young Americans died there for reasons that a significant segment of the American population didn't support. Combatants on both sides

> *Never have nations of the world had so much to lose or so much to gain. Together we shall save our planet or together we shall perish in its flames. Save it we can and save it we must, and then shall we earn the eternal thanks of mankind and, as peacemakers, the eternal blessing of God.*
> John F. Kennedy
> Former U.S. President

accused each other (as they do in all wars) of aggression and crimes against humanity. After careful deliberation, I decided that I would gradually withdraw from the private practice of law and would dedicate myself to studying and writing about world peace.

True loyalty does not demand blind obedience. "My country right or wrong" is a prescription for national decay. As the Germans under Hitler learned, it could be a recipe for disaster.

Citizenship and true patriotism carry a duty to encourage your country when it is right and to help it when it has gone astray. I was determined to try to make my adopted country more responsive to the needs and aspirations of all its citizens so that it could remain a continuing inspiration to the peoples of the world.

BOOKS FOR PEACE

My book, *Defining International Aggression—The Search for World Peace*, was published in 1975. It seemed to me that there was little sense in denouncing aggression, terrorism, and other crimes against humanity unless these offenses became part of an accepted international criminal code enforced by an international court. I wrote another two-volume documentary history, *An International Criminal Court—A Step Toward World Peace*, that was published in 1980. It was intended to be a tool which nations could use to build a structure for peace.

> The central task of our time is to evolve a new system of world order based on principles of peace and justice.
> Richard Falk, 1983
> Professor of Law, Princeton University

While still at Harvard, I had studied jurisprudence with Professor Roscoe Pound, one of the most learned jurists in the world. In the back of my mind, his wise teaching remained. He believed that *no regime could be considered lawful unless it contained three components: codes, courts, and enforcement.* To complete the trilogy, I needed to study the problem of enforcement. So back I went to the libraries and U.N. meetings.

Three floors beneath the U.N. building in New York are the archives of the League of Nations. Here there are thousands of old books dealing with war and peace. I obtained a key to the rooms in which these treasures were kept. For long days and nights I sat there alone probing the wisdom of many scholars *who had devoted their minds to the greatest problem that still vexed humankind.* The results of my research were recorded in another two-volume book, *Enforcing International Law—A Way to World Peace*, that was published in 1983.

My books were intended primarily for university libraries, government officials, professors of law or political science, and policymakers of all nations. The six volumes contain the details and documents to show that a world of international law, courts, and effective enforcement is both necessary and feasible as we move into the 21st Century. In order to spread the word to a larger audience, I condensed the gist of my thinking into a small inexpensive paperback, *A Common Sense Guide to World Peace*. The title was influenced by that great patriot, Tom Paine, whose pamphlet *Common Sense* had inspired the American revolution. On October 25, 1985, I sent the first copies to President Reagan and General Secretary Gorbachev of the Soviet Union.

Like Tom Paine, *I hoped my writing would serve the interests of humanity*. My little book on world peace was respectfully dedicated:

> To those leaders of the United States and the Soviet Union who will have the courage and the wisdom to overcome their fears and reconcile their differences, so that all who dwell on this planet may live together in peace and dignity regardless of their race or creed.

When the two world leaders met at the summit in Washington, D.C. in December 1987, they were able to sign an agreement to destroy all of the intermediate range nuclear weapons. This reduced the nuclear arsenal by four percent. They spoke of a nuclear free world in the future. They had finally begun "to overcome their fears and reconcile their differences."

However, political leaders cannot act in a vacuum. They need support or prodding from an informed public. The people must be educated and encouraged to speak out for a world system of lasting peace and abundance. This book was written to help them move rapidly toward this supreme goal.

1st Step

Insist
on Your
Ultimate
Human
Right

The ancient Greeks had a legend about a nice guy named Damocles who sat down to enjoy a great feast. The table was loaded with all known delicacies. Everything was perfect—except for one thing. Suspended above his head was a sharp-pointed sword held by only a single hair! THIS IS YOU AND ME TODAY!

We live in a world in which many people enjoy comfortable living conditions that even a monarch of old could not duplicate—TV, air conditioning, automobiles, health care, etc. Yet we greatly limit our prosperity and threaten our future with the way we run the planet today, *wasting $1.5 million every minute* on mass killing machines. According to a 1987 issue of *The Defense Monitor*, "Preparations for war have cost the United States $2 trillion since 1981. This amounts to $21,000 for each American household."

> *Our world is prodigiously healthy and vigorous, and terribly sick at the same time. The extraordinary upsurge and economic expansion of the past fifteen years . . . give hope of unprecedented progress and welfare. The malady that may destroy everybody, and everything is caused exclusively by our totally outdated political institutions—in flagrant contradiction to the economic and technological realities of our time.*
>
> Emery Reves
> *The Anatomy of Peace*

The incredible thing about our lives going into the 21st Century is that we stand on the threshold of an enormous increase of good things beyond the levels of the past or present: potentially more freedom, security, education, material comfort, and entertainment to mention only a few—and yet we have a nuclear sword of Damocles suspended by a hair over our heads. We could die at any time in a nuclear war begun by accident or deliberately started by a fanatic.

PlanetHood is your personal how-to-do-it instruction book. It spells out how you can give yourself and your family a life of lasting peace and *unparalleled personal prosperity*. This book explains the eight positive steps you can begin taking immediately to create a world with a wonderful future.

In spite of all the gloom and doom of our nuclear predicament, *PlanetHood* offers you a wonderful, life-enriching solution. There is a clear-cut, effective way in which "the scourge of war" can be forever removed from this earth!!! This book presents a solution that has 200 years of successful testing to prove that it really works!

INTERNATIONAL ANARCHY

We live today in a world of increasing international anarchy. Most nations are loading up with all the killing machines they can afford—*or can't afford.* Five nations now acknowledge having nuclear weapons (U.S., Soviet Union, England, France, China), and 52 nations have nuclear research facilities. According to Charles Ebinger of Georgetown University's Center for Strategic and International Studies, "It's probably the most pessimistic issue I've ever dealt with. Nobody seems to come up with any solutions, myself included."

> *With all my heart I believe that the world's present system of sovereign nations can lead only to barbarism, war and inhumanity.*
>
> Albert Einstein

The U.S. military has developed a 58-pound nuclear "backpack" bomb that can be carried by one person. The principles for building nuclear bombs are known throughout the world. Do you want your children to live in a world in which only one "terrorist" or "freedom fighter" can kill more people in an hour than a whole army in the past?

Dr. Yevgeny I. Chazov, Deputy Minister of Health of the U.S.S.R. and cardiologist to leaders in the Kremlin, pleads with us, "We must preserve our life on earth. We must struggle for the survival of our children and grandchildren. People of all political outlooks, nationalities, and religions must urge their governments to concentrate their attention not on what steps to take to attain victory in nuclear war, but on

> *The bulk of nuclear weapons is concentrated in the Soviet Union and the United States. Meanwhile, ten percent or even one percent of their potential is enough to inflict irreparable damage on our planet and all human civilization . . . . We and the Americans bear the greatest responsibility toward the world's nations. Our two countries and peoples and their politicians bear a special, unique responsibility to all human civilization.*
>
> Mikhail Gorbachev
> Soviet General Secretary
> *Perestroika: New Thinking for Our Country and the World*

what must be done so that the flames of such a war will never burn on our planet." As a medical man (and with Dr. Bernard Lown, a Nobel Peace Prize winner and cofounder of the International Physicians for the Prevention of Nuclear War), Dr. Chazov has asked, "You come to us to save your children. Why, when we ask you to help us save mankind, are you indifferent?"

According to Rear Admiral Gene R. LaRocque, U.S. Navy (Ret.), "It's very important for all of us today to realize that the Soviet Union is not the enemy. Nuclear war is the enemy. We're going to have to learn to live with the Russians or we and the Russians are going to die at about the same time."*

---

*Admiral LaRocque is the Director of the Center for Defense Information, 1500 Massachusetts Avenue, N.W., Washington, D.C. 20005. Phone: (202) DEFENSE. You may wish to contact the Center for a copy of its informative periodical, *The Defense Monitor*.

28

Summing up our incredible predicament, the United States and the Soviet Union spend a combined total of more than $500 billion per year on armaments. There are over 50,000 nuclear devices on Earth with an explosive capacity of 15,000 to 20,000 million tons of TNT. Since the world population is just over 5 billion, that works out to an average of 3 to 4 TONS of TNT waiting to kill each man, woman, and child on Earth!

DISARMAMENT ALONE WON'T WORK

Like others all over the world, we welcomed the Intermediate-range Nuclear Treaty signed by Reagan and Gorbachev in December 1987. Subject to the approval of the Senate, it offers a *four percent* reduction of the deadly nuclear arsenal of our two nations. It was an important first step toward halting the arms race. *However, we must not be lulled into complacency by thinking we can build a secure, peaceful world through disarmament alone.*

Disarmament only affects some of the *symptoms* of the cancer of war: the killing machinery. It does not in any way get rid of the cancer itself: settling disagreements by war. This cancer will eventually kill us if we don't do something about it. We must not be hypnotized into a false confidence that disarmament alone solves the problem of war.

Most of us are delighted that an entire class of intermediate-range nuclear weapons is to be wiped out of the arsenals of at least two nations. However, as long as

> *Unless some effective supranational government can be set up and brought quickly into action, the prospects of peace and human progress are dark and doubtful.*
> Winston Churchill
> Former British Prime Minister

the generals and admirals in the Pentagon and Kremlin have the responsibility for protecting their nation

through military clout, *we are still stuck in a war system.* Did you hear any suggestion by the U.S. government that reducing nuclear arms by four percent lets us lower the military budget by four percent? Quite the contrary! The Pentagon promptly demanded increases for conventional weapons. Even if we reduced our weapons by fifty percent, there is no doubt that military planners would demand a higher budget to kill people in other nations by other means. We still think in narrow national terms. We must begin to think in planetary terms if we are to find peace.

Let's suppose all nuclear weapons were removed from the face of the earth through 100% nuclear disarmament by all the 159 nations of this world. *Humanity would still be in trouble.* The killing technology of today, even with non-nuclear weapons, is *far more deadly* than anything used during World War II until Hiroshima and Nagasaki. The ingenuity of the human mind

> *The splitting of the atom has changed everything, save our mode of thinking, and thus we drift toward unparalleled catastrophe.*
>
> Albert Einstein

is discovering even cheaper ways of killing off people in other nations when we disagree with their leaders. At least 16 nations today already have what *Time* magazine has called "the poor man's atomic bomb." Today's nerve gas can produce fever and uncontrolled vomiting that will be followed by paralysis and death by asphyxiation. According to the American Chemical Association, the Pentagon already has five thousand times enough nerve gas to kill everyone on earth. The Kremlin can probably match the U.S. sniff by sniff.

But let's be super optimists and suppose that a miracle of disarmament happens. Let's imagine that all nations on earth strip themselves of all armaments—*both nuclear and conventional*—and these are completely destroyed by the end of this century. Will humanity now be safe? No! The technological information that enables us to build efficient killing machines cannot be destroyed. When the people who engineered this hypothetical disarmament miracle are *no longer in office,* politicians with less goodwill (or more hunger for power) could easily reactivate the arms race. That's what Hitler did. If only one nation begins a new arms race, everyone else has to "defend" themselves by following suit.

We feel like party poopers when we warn you that disarmament alone can be dangerously misleading if it creates an illusion that we've solved the problem of war. Disarmament was popular after the first World War (in which 10 million people were killed and 20 million wounded). Some armaments were scrapped and limitations were agreed on. In the 1930's Soviet Foreign Minister Maxim Litvinov proposed that we have total disarmament. The public was tranquilized by the *apparent* progress. Then the reality of World War II hit the world in 1939. After all this wonderful disarmament of the 20's and 30's, World War II killed some 35 million human beings, injured and maimed millions more, destroyed billions of dollars worth of property, and disrupted countless lives on this planet.

MORE GUNS WON'T WORK

Another approach to world peace that sincere people are still trying to get to work is that of arming their country to the teeth under the theory of deterrence—often called "mutual assured destruction" (MAD). However, as Emery Reves pointed out, *one person's deterrence is another's incentive to start an arms race!* That's what has happened to the U.S. and the Soviet Union in the last forty years.

Since a nuclear missile can travel anywhere on earth in about 30 minutes, the warning time is now so short that it is possible for a war to be started by a computer malfunction that is misinterpreted. Computers and warning systems have been known to give false alarms. Space debris such as meteors or satellites reentering the atmosphere can be mistaken for a missile attack—especially when tension is high.

> *Betting on deterrence to continue to save us from nuclear annihilation is like building your house on the side of a volcano and hoping it will never erupt.*
> Tom Hudgens
> *Let's Abolish War*

Do you want the life of your family to terminate because of a computer error?

When we rely on killing machines, absolute security for one nation must mean absolute insecurity for all the rest. Year by year the increasing proliferation of armaments, and the training of men and women to kill each other, encourages a more and more violent world. Poor

> *The ideology of deterrence must not receive the church's blessing, even as a temporary warrant for holding on to nuclear weapons.*
>
> Pastoral Letter of
> Methodist Bishops, 1986

third world nations may not be able to afford food, education, or health care, but they've got lots of guns. More guns are not a workable way to achieve permanent world peace.

Some people hope that the Star Wars "shield" would save us. Knowledgeable military and scientific experts say that it can't possibly protect us against nuclear catastrophe. Step Six spells out the misleading way Star Wars is being explained to the American people.

WAR WITHOUT A WINNER

This is not a book on nuclear horror. We do not wish to belabor the nuclear peril in which humanity finds itself today. We must, however, present one more overview before we proceed with the **eight positive steps** that you can begin taking immediately to move toward a new era of planethood in which we no longer use killing machines to solve disagreements between nations.

Since Hiroshima, military power isn't what it used to be. World War II was the last major war that will ever be "won" by superior power. There can be no winner in a nuclear war—only losers. Scientist Carl Sagan has pointed out that if either the U.S. or the Soviet Union launches an all-out first strike with nuclear missiles, *and the other side does not fire back a single shot in retaliation,* the nuclear winter effect causing the lowering of planetary light and temperature and other lethal consequences will wipe out human life not only in the targeted nation but also in the aggressor nation and throughout most of the earth!!!*

Today the populations of both superpowers are in effect held as mutual hostages under the threat of imminent extinction by blast, fire, or lingering death by radiation and nuclear winter. Within a day or two, the superpowers could fire about 6,000 times the quantities of explosives that were fired over the entire four years of World War II! It is sheer folly to try to protect the world by threatening to destroy it.

RESCUING YOURSELF AND YOUR FAMILY

The only sure way to give you, your family, and all of us a future on this earth (plus unparalleled abundance) is to rapidly achieve a new international system in which we fight our battles in the courtroom instead of the killing fields. And this is the central message of *PlanetHood*: we can and must replace the law of force with the

> *After the first exchange of missiles . . . the ashes of Communism and the ashes of Capitalism will be indistinguishable.*
> John Kenneth Galbraith
> Noted Economist

force of law internationally. The eight steps in this book will show you how you can help it happen soon.**

"A nuclear war cannot be won," said President Reagan, "and must never be fought." The words sound fine—but somehow the accompanying music doesn't seem right. We cannot depend upon our politicians to save us. Politicians are usually dedicated

---

The Cold and the Dark: The World After Nuclear War by Paul R. Ehrlich, Carl Sagan, Donald Kennedy, Walter Orr Roberts. New York: W.W. Norton & Company, 1984.

**Appendix 3 contains a *Reader's Digest* condensation of *The Anatomy of Peace* by Emery Reves. It brilliantly presents the exact cause and practical cure for war.

to protecting their separate partisan, parochial, or local interests as they perceive them. The thinking habits of many of them tend toward the old style of defense: if you want peace, prepare for war. They usually rely on the old jungle law that says might makes right. They do not appear to really understand that killing machines are now the enemy—not the savior—of their people.

Reason tells us that if the mortal mind is able to invent devices powerful enough to destroy the world, it must also be capable of devising a world system to prevent its destruction. My feelings tell me that *optimism and individual effort are essential* if the problems of world peace are to be solved.

Without optimism that human betterment is possible, despondency and despair would destroy the initiative and determination that are needed to defeat the prophecies of doom. Hope is the motor that drives human endeavor. Only through confidence in the future can humankind muster the courage and strength to do what is required for survival. We have, therefore, deliberately chosen to view the glass as half-full rather than half-empty.

> *We have a choice. Humanity either can learn to manage the risks of living together under a law system or can prepare to die together under the war system.*
> Myron W. Kronisch
> Campaign for U.N. Reform

But we are also convinced that *optimism is justified by the facts.* Despite all of the contemporary stresses and strife, an objective analysis of the historical record will show that humankind is experiencing a continuous—though wobbly—movement toward a more cooperative world order. The powerful growth described in this book must be nurtured with care if it is to reach maturity. *We must not be tempted to abandon the baby just because it was not born full grown.*

So you're going to have to do the job of saving yourself—and all of humanity. *Your survival is too important to trust to anyone else.* It's a do-it-yourself job for all of us on earth—and time is short. No one knows how long we have.

OUR ULTIMATE HUMAN RIGHT

It is obvious that the time has come for "we the people" of the world to prevent our own annihilation. To help us rescue ourselves, the senior author has formulated a proclamation of our ultimate human right that can act as a rallying call:

I have the right to live in a peaceful world free from the threat of death by nuclear war.

We must strongly assert our ultimate human right in ways that our military and political leaders can hear—firmly, caringly, and *nonviolently*. To fall into the trap of violence in the cause of nonviolence and peace is simply perpetuating the old habits of thinking that have put us into our present predicament.

The people on this earth do not want to be killed through nuclear war—or any other kind of war. Mothers, fathers, and children have suffered far too much from the recurrent wars that have plagued human history for thousands of years. Unfortunately when many of these same people acquire positions of military and political power in the governments of the world, they fall into the trap of thinking that killing power equals security. Today this is small-brain dinosaur thinking.

> *It is high time for humanity to accept and work out the full consequences of the total global and interdependent nature of our planetary home and of our species. Our survival and further progress will depend largely on the advent of global visions and of proper global education in all countries of the world.*
>
> Robert Muller, 1982
> Author and U.N. Assistant. Secy.-Gen.

The first step that you can take to rescue yourself from nuclear extinction is to clearly assert our *ultimate human right* to live in a world free from the threat of death by nuclear war. This right is termed "ultimate," for unless we can make the transition from the *law of force* to the *force of law*, all of our other rights will remain in jeopardy. Our right to human dignity, to practice the faith of our choice, to earn a living, have decent housing, food, medical care, and the "pursuit of happiness," are *meaningless* if there are no human beings on earth to enjoy these rights! Whatever religious, economic, social, political, or other benefits we wish to enjoy, all will be lost unless we rapidly secure our *ultimate human right*.

IT'S YOUR BIRTHRIGHT

This proclamation of our basic human right is not something invented out of thin air. It has been developing as part of the growing respect for the rights of all individuals. *This ultimate human right upon which all other human rights depend can only be protected by replacing international lawlessness with enforced international law.*

The United Nations Charter confirms the determination of all nations "to save succeeding generations from the scourge of war." The Universal Declaration of Human Rights adopted in 1948 by the U.N. declares that "everyone has the right to life, liberty and security of person" and refers to "a social order and international order" in which those rights "can be fully realized." These civil, political, economic, social, and cultural rights have been promised to all humankind.

Without peace, no human right is secure. The monetary and human cost of preparing for war (usually called "defense") makes it impossible to fully attain our declared human rights. The threat of nuclear warfare places all living things in mortal peril. It is appropriate,

> *The problem in defense is how far you can go without destroying from within what you are trying to defend from without.*
> Dwight D. Eisenhower
> January 18, 1953
> Former U.S. President

therefore, that the ultimate human right be clearly articulated and proclaimed as the supreme goal for the remaining years of the 20th Century. The guardian of all of our hopes, dreams, and truths resides in our ultimate human right to live in a peaceful world free from the threat of death by nuclear war.

YOUR FIRST STEP TO PLANETHOOD

Your first step toward planethood is to assert your ultimate right as a human being who shares our common planet. We hope a proclamation of the ultimate human right will be signed by every concerned citizen throughout the world. It should be posted on the walls of our offices and factories, made visually available in every home, printed on billboards, taught in every school, and written in the sky.

Appendix 4 contains copies of this proclamation you can use in signing up your friends and neighbors. When each sheet is filled out, it should be sent to Mr. Javier Pérez de Cuéllar, Secretary-General of the United Nations, with a request that he inform the nations of the world what we, the people, are demanding. You can begin to let people know you're fed up with the way the world is being run.

As we mentioned, there are eight specific steps YOU can take to make this ultimate human right a living reality for yourself and everyone. In the following pages, we will outline what many years of intensive study tells us will work. We offer it only as a frame of reference. Others may approach the problems of world peace from a different perspective. We welcome that. The more people ponder these vital problems, the sooner wise solutions will be found.

> *If we do not want to die together in war, we must learn to live together in peace.*
>
> Harry S. Truman, 1945
> Former U.S. President

By taking this first step, you are beginning to insist on your ultimate human right. You are now ready to consider the second step (explained in the next section) to secure your right to live in a peaceful and prosperous world free from the threat of death by nuclear war—and to benefit by the exciting new era the 21st Century offers us.

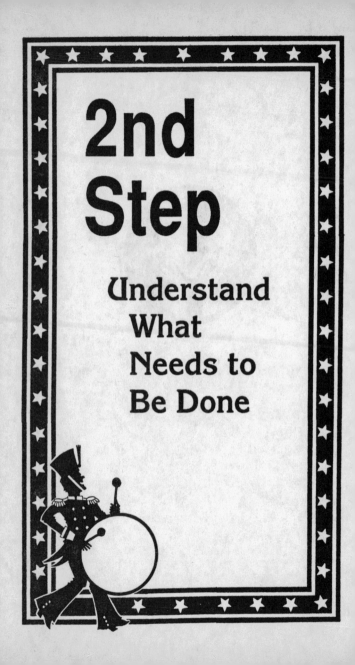

2nd Step

Understand What Needs to Be Done

There'll always be a bad guy hanging out in the international neighborhood as long as we have an ungoverned world of anarchy and lawlessness. This book describes the way to save humanity from the perpetual warfare that squeezes us to pay for killing machines and deprives us of planetary prosperity. And it doesn't depend on everyone becoming nice and kind by tomorrow!

> *We must create world-wide law and law enforcement as we outlaw world-wide war and weapons.*
>
> John F. Kennedy
> Former U.S. President

Unless we change our ways, humanity seems headed toward eventual death. Some new approach is needed to give our children a future! How do we switch from the arms race to a peace race? What can we do about the gravest crisis humanity has ever faced?

SOLVING THE PROBLEM OF WAR

The only way to permanently solve the problem of war between nations is to replace the LAW OF FORCE with the FORCE OF LAW.

40

Laying aside all the jokes we love to tell about our politicians, *we've developed systems for governing ourselves that really work!* You probably slept soundly in your bed last night because your city has a system of laws, enforcement, and courts that make you relatively safe. (Bear in mind that nothing's perfect—we are talking about practicalities.) Similarly, the state in which you live has a political structure that provides the three elements needed for adequate government: elected representatives to make laws, an executive branch with police to enforce the laws, and courts to fairly resolve disputes, decide who's innocent, who's broken the law, and what their punishment will be.

> ... they shall beat their swords into plowshares, and their spears into pruning hooks; nations shall not lift up sword against nation, neither shall they learn war any more.
>
> The Bible, Micah 4:3

Without these three elements—*laws, enforcement, and courts*—lawlessness will reign. You might have to kill or risk being killed just to provide yourself with a lower level of safety than your city, county, and state governments are now giving you. Remember the Wild West of the last century in which anyone with a pistol could act as a lawmaker, enforcer, judge, jury, and executioner—sometimes all within one minute? The bloodshed of the Wild West days finally forced us to tighten law and order. Similarly, the constant killing and the nuclear threat to wipe out all human life can force the nations of this earth to go beyond today's primitive way of solving disputes by mass murder.

FORCE IS UNNECESSARY

A workable alternative to the use of force requires many innovations. The United Nations and similar organizations for international cooperation and settling disputes must be vastly improved. National arms must be brought under international controls. Self-help through warlike actions must be replaced by a system of coordinated economic sanctions supported by the resources of the world community. An International Peace Force must be created as the ultimate law enforcement agency.

Those who are expected to comply with such a design for international law and order must be convinced that the laws are as fair as can be expected. They must recognize that the objective of the system is not the exploitation of the weak or the preservation of privilege for the powerful. No

> *Abolition of war is no longer an ethical question to be pondered solely by learned philosophers and ecclesiastics, but a hard core one for the decision of the masses whose survival is the issue. Many will tell you with mockery and ridicule that the abolition of war can only be a dream . . . that it is the vague imagining of a visionary. But we must go on or we will go under! We must have new thoughts, new ideas, new concepts. We must break out of the straitjacket of the past. We must have sufficient imaginations and courage to translate the universal wish for peace—which is rapidly becoming a universal necessity—into actuality.*
>
> Douglas MacArthur
> U.S. General

system of law can be enforced if it does not have as its most vital ingredient the goal of social justice for the entire human community.*

JUST ONE MORE LAYER

Today in the United States, we have four layers of government: city, county, state, and national. We have these four layers because we need them to avoid anarchy *within our nation*. It's inspiring to know that *adding only one more layer of government* will enable us to have an abundant future on this planet.

International governance—something like a United Nations of the World—will rescue us from our deadly predicament. U.S. President Harry S. Truman in his down-to-earth way said, "When Kansas and Colorado have a quarrel over water in the

*All of this is spelled out in *Enforcing International Law—A Way to World Peace* by Benjamin B. Ferencz. 2 volumes. New York: Oceana Publications, 1983. Available in many university libraries.

Arkansas River, they don't call out the National Guard in each state and go to war over it. They bring suit in the Supreme Court

> *Mankind's desire for peace can be realized only by the creation of a world government.*
>
> Albert Einstein

of the United States and abide by the decision. There isn't a reason in the world why we cannot do that internationally. . . . It will be just as easy for nations to get along in a republic of the world as it is for you to get along in the republic of the United States."

The gradual growth of international law and cooperation over the past century has set the stage for us to create a permanent peace with worldwide prosperity. Let's look at the progress we have made in replacing the *law of force* with the *force of law*. Louis Sohn, Professor of International Law, Emeritus, Harvard Law School, has pointed out that in the last

> . . . forty years more international agreements have been concluded than during the previous four millennia; that the International Court of Justice after a period of unemployment has now more cases than it can comfortably handle (including several cases testifying to its acceptance by the African countries and other new members of the international community); that several regional and functional courts are dealing with a rapidly increasing number of cases; and that more than two hundred international organizations deal with matters of daily concern to the majority of mankind in such an efficient and smooth way that their activities are generally accepted without a murmur.*

This wonderful progress can now become a foundation for a lawful world.

You'll be amazed at how much has already been done. According to Willy Brandt, former Chancellor of West

*From Professor Sohn's Introduction to *A Common Sense Guide to World Peace* by Benjamin B. Ferencz. New York: Oceana Publications, 1985.

Germany, "The Federal Republic of Germany [in becoming a member of the European Community] has declared in its Constitution its willingness to transfer sovereign rights to supernational organizations and it has placed international law above national law .... This expresses the realization that the sovereignty of the individual and of nations can be secured only in larger communities."

Many other constitutions and treaties drawn up in recent years provide for some subordination of national government to an international system of law and order. Among these are the constitutions of Belgium, France, Costa Rica, India, Italy, Japan, Luxembourg, and

> *This statement is for all those who fear that it is unpatriotic to have a government greater than their own. There is no greater patriotic duty than to preserve your own nation and its freedoms. It is true that we must retain our freedoms when we unite into one federation, except for the freedom to make war. Just as our own 50 states have turned over this task to our national government, so the 160 nations, or however many join, must turn over warmaking and defense to the world federation. I live in Cherry Hills, Colorado, and I think it is the finest city in the world. I live in Arapahoe County, and I think it is the finest county in the world. I live in the state of Colorado, and I think it is the greatest state in the world. I live in the United States of America, and I think it is the greatest country in the world. But I also live on Planet Earth, and it does not detract one iota from my patriotism to my city, my county, my state, and my country for me to feel that this planet is the greatest in the universe and that I will defend it against all perils to the best of my ability. What we need in this world is a pledge of allegiance to Planet Earth by every citizen of the world.*
>
> Tom A. Hudgens
> *Let's Abolish War*

Norway. It is interesting to note that Article Nine of the 1947 Japanese Constitution, instituted while MacArthur was its leader, states that Japan " . . . forever renounces war as a sovereign right of a nation, and the threat or use of force as means of settling international disputes." Japan has been the richer for its decision.

To give ourselves the peace and abundance of planethood, *we must enlarge our idea of patriotism.* George Washington also faced the problem of limited loyalty. For example, during the war for American independence one woman wrote, "Washington tried to persuade his New Jersey troops to swear allegiance to the United States. They refused. 'New Jersey is our country!' they said stubbornly." In the Continental Congress a New Jersey member denounced the General's action as improper. *Our patriotism must be enlarged one more step to the international level for the common good of all humanity.*

> *Internationalism does not mean the end of individual nations. Orchestras don't mean the end of violins.*
> Golda Meir
> Prime Minister of Israel

If we work as hard to promote a world republic as we do to sell cola drinks in every country, we can achieve a lawful world free from the threat of war before the end of this century. *PlanetHood* is an idea whose time has come.

INTERNATIONAL "WILD WEST" MUST END

In the days of the Wild West, people wore guns on their hips to "protect" themselves. Any barroom dispute could end in killing. Outlaws ran wild. The death rate without law and order was much too high. To create peaceful communities, the citizens demanded sheriffs and courts to enforce laws—not just every man for himself. We must now do this internationally.

Today no world legislature exists to decree what each country may or may not do. There is no executive branch to enforce international laws, and no world court making *binding* decisions based on an International Constitution. As matters now stand, nations decide for themselves how to handle conflicts. They pick which versions of ambiguous agreements they will follow.

Many agreements have been accepted by the world community to stipulate the bounds of permissible international behavior. But almost all such instruments contain artfully constructed clauses *deliberately formulated with such skillful ambiguity* as to allow each nation to interpret the vague phrases to its advantage! *Any system that allows competing parties to interpret laws primarily on the basis of their own advantage is unworthy of respect; it is practically no legal system at all.*

In 1979, for example, 118 nations voted for an International Convention Against the Taking of Hostages. Any party apprehending an offender was obliged "without exception whatsoever" to prosecute or extradite the criminal. Despite this seemingly comprehensive language, exceptions were put in which gave sanctuary to those who acted for political motives or who were fighting against "colonial domination and alien occupation" or "in the exercise of their right of self-determination."

> *We are convinced that a comprehensive system of security is at the same time a system of universal law and order ensuring the primacy of international law in politics . . . .*
>
> Mikhail Gorbachev
> Soviet General Secreatry
> Article in *Pravda*
> September 17, 1987

The same loopholes appeared in agreements against other acts of terrorism. Under such circumstances of legal double talk, it should surprise no one that acts of terrorism have continued.

The definition of aggression is so riddled with contradictory clauses that it is all but ignored by the Security Council of the United Nations which is supposed to be guided by it. Binding treaties, signed to keep the skies free of ballistic missiles, are later interpreted in ways that defeat the fundamental purposes of the agreement.

If laws are designed with loopholes, lawbreakers will use the loopholes to do as they please. Those who wish to live under the protection of law cannot be allowed to evade the law through self-serving misinterpretations.

THREE ALTERNATIVES

A planetary system must be set up so that it is *not too powerful* (thus avoiding tyranny) *and not too weak* (thus avoiding ineffectiveness). There are three basic ways to create an international governance—ranging from bad to good:

1. A World Dictatorship. An awful way to get rid of world anarchy is to set up a world system with a powerful world dictator or international king of all countries. The history of dictators like Hitler warns us that *power must be limited.* Lord Acton in 1887 observed, "Power tends to corrupt; absolute power corrupts absolutely." Strong checks and balances are essential to prevent concentrated power in the hands of one person—or one special interest. A world dictatorship is definitely *not* the solution we are seeking; it would be like jumping out of the frying pan into the fire.

2. A Confederation of Nations. A confederation sounds good on paper but in practice it just doesn't work. The United Nations today is a confederation of 159 sovereign nations. With good intentions its Charter begins, "We the Peoples of the United Nations determined to save succeeding generations from the scourge of war . . . ." The U.N. has a General Assembly (in which each nation has one vote), a Security Council, and a World Court at The Hague. Unfortunately, like our Articles of Confederation written over two centuries ago, the Charter can't work to prevent all wars because it's too weak.

> *One reason nations go to war (there are 40 wars now going on around the world) is because at times they have no other place to go. Contending parties can become so locked into rigid positions that squaring off in blood seems the only alternative.*
>
> Eric Cox
> Campaign for U.N. Reform

Today's U.N. is still stuck in a war system! When Iran grabbed the American Embassy and held its people as hostages, the U.S. went to the World Court at The Hague. It decided unanimously in favor of the U.S. *However, there is no enforcement of court decisions!* So the hostages remained prisoners. When the United States mined a Nicaraguan harbor and Nicaragua filed a complaint, the U.S. rejected the court's jurisdiction. World protests were ignored when Soviet troops were sent to Afghanistan. The usual anarchy attitude is: *either accept our illegal actions—or go to war*. We've built so many loopholes into the U.N. system that it is helpless to prevent aggression unless we reform the U.N. Charter.

The Charter was deliberately made weak so that no one could tell anyone else what to do. We made it impotent and—by giving five powerful nations the right to veto any enforcement action—*deliberately left open the option of settling disputes by war.* In spite of the high ideals in the Charter and its prohibition against the use of force (except in self-defense), we did not give the United Nations the binding strength needed to get rid of international lawlessness.

The U.N. has, however, been a valuable and necessary step in setting the stage for a more workable international governance. It's now time to reform the U.N. into an effective vehicle for peaceful planethood.

3. A World Democratic Republic. A democratic republic of the world will complete our governmental structure to fill our urgent need. All nations on the earth can be protected by an international constitution providing for an international congress to pass laws, an international court to apply the laws, and an international executive branch to enforce the laws. Our representatives to the world congress would protect us in a way that we lack

> *It is time to stop patronizing the people. It is time to stop treating them as children. Peace people are very good at telling us how dangerous the arms race is. It is dangerous, very, very dangerous. We should continue to stress that. But we should also find the courage to tell people how radical the necessary remedy for the arms race is and why that radical remedy is necessary.*
>
> Dr. John Logue
> Director, Common Heritage Institute

today. We can achieve our "planethood" through a United Nations of the world—just as we achieved our nationhood through the Constitution of the United States of America.*

---

* See *World Peace Through World Law* by Grenville Clark and Louis B. Sohn. 3rd ed. Cambridge: Harvard University Press, 1966. A basic book describing reforms needed to make the U.N. effective.

ESSENTIALS OF A WORLD CONSTITUTION

1. A Bill of Rights.
2. A popularly elected legislature to enact world laws.
3. A world court to interpret those laws, with compulsory jurisdiction over world disputes.
4. A civilian executive branch with the power to enforce world laws directly upon individuals.
5. A system of checks and balances to prevent the abuse of power by any branch of the world government.
6. The control of all weapons of mass destruction by the world government, with the disarmament of all nations, under careful inspection down to the level required for internal policing.
7. Carefully defined and limited power of taxation to support those functions necessary to world peace and the solution of problems affecting, to a vital degree, the welfare of all mankind.
8. Reasonable provision for amendments.
9. Participation in the world federal government to be open at all times to all nations.
10. All power not expressly delegated to the world government to be reserved to the nations and their peoples, thus leaving each nation to choose its own political, social, and economic systems.

From the American Movement for World Government, One World Trade Center, Suite 7967, New York, NY 10048.

LIMITING POWER

We must *limit the power* of a world system in the way our founding fathers limited the power of the United States Government. We must use checks and balances to avoid the pitfalls of power. We must provide the people of the world with peace and dignity through international law enforced by an executive branch and a world judiciary.

The U.S. Constitution left all power in the hands of the individual states except for matters involving other states or nations. Disagreements between states are settled legally—not lethally—by U.S. laws, courts, and executive enforcement. *Because of the wise checks and balances that limit the power of Congress, the Supreme Court, and the executive branch, no king or dictator can get control of the government of the United States.*

To save all of humanity from nuclear death and set the stage for worldwide prosperity, we can use a governmental structure similar to the one that for over two centuries has made the United States one of the most prosperous and strongest nations on earth.

> *I have long believed the only way peace can be achieved is through World Government.*
>
> Jawaharal Nehru
> Former Prime Minister of India

U.S. citizens are given enormous individual rights—bearing in mind that my right to swing my arms freely ends where your nose begins! We have a successful model that can work in the international area just as it has worked for the United States in the national area.

SAFELY DISARMING!

When we are protected by international laws, courts, and effective enforcement, we can at last safely disarm this bristling world. This would include destroying all mass killing machines. *Those deadly bombers, missiles, tanks, submarines, and battleships are not needed to maintain law and order inside a nation.*

No more armies, navies, air forces, or Star Wars! No international arms trade. They wouldn't be needed.

The United Nations would instead have a staff of well-trained and equipped air and ground peace-keeping forces to keep order among the nation-states of the world. Think of all the money and lives this would save! Instead of many millions of soldiers in national armies *that have not kept world order*, a few hundred thousand world "policemen" could preserve planetary law and order. And the price is right!

> *I am convinced that the Great Framer of the World will so develop it that it becomes one nation, so that armies and navies are no longer necessary .... I believe at some future day, the nations of the earth will agree upon some sort of congress which will take cognizance of international questions of difficulty and whose decisions will be as binding as the decisions of our Supreme Court are upon us.*
>
> Ulysses S. Grant
> U.S. President, 1869-1877

INTERNAL FREEDOM TO CHOOSE

We don't want the ways of other nations forced on us, and we must understandably avoid trying to push our economic, social, religious, or political forms on other countries. The U.S. Constitution wisely limits the legislative power of the Federal Government to interstate matters. Similarly a World Constitution must allow the people of the world to run their own countries. Capitalist nations can remain capitalistic; communist nations can remain communistic. Each nation could determine for itself how to run its own economy and politics. The goal is international unity—not national uniformity. Unity with diversity!

While the reformed United Nations organization would have a democratic voting system and the right to pass binding laws, the 159 individual nation-states would continue to choose their own forms of government. Thus, Saudi Arabia has a king; many countries have presidents that were not elected by the people; England has a parliamentary system based on both heredity and popular vote; Sweden and Iceland could remain Socialistic; the Soviet Union may remain Communistic; and some countries have federal republics like the United States. If individual nations wish to hold onto or change their way of governing themselves, it's their own business.

Many sincere people are deeply concerned about the spread of Communism throughout the world. Is it safe to have a world government that would allow other forms of government including those that might try to spread their dominion over other nations? YES, IT IS SAFE! It is a hundred times safer than our situation today!!!

The international peacekeeping forces and the World Court would have the power to stop any nation from illegally using armed force or military threats to coerce the people of any other nation in any way at any time in any form. Grievances could be brought before the World Court whose decisions would be binding. An International Congress, World Court, and en-

> *You cannot erect a peace system on a basis of the coercion of governments by governments, because that is trying to build a peace system on a foundation of war. The only basis for a peace system is a pooling of sovereignty for supernational purposes, that is the creation of a common nationhood, above but entirely separate from the diverse local nationhoods.*
>
> Philip Henry Kerr
> Marquis of Lothian
> Burge Memorial Lecture, 1935

forcement branch could keep the nations of the world *far safer in preserving their traditions than they are today.* There is no safety in today's world. Through enforced world law, all nations can be safe!

Can a nation try to convince other nations to do as it does? Yes. Using the international right of free speech guaranteed by the World Constitution, the U.S. will be free to try to convince other nations to adopt its political and economic forms; Sweden and Iceland can try to persuade other nations to adopt a socialistic economy, and Saudi Arabia may choose to recommend to other nations that they use a kingly form. And the Soviet Union can use its right of free international speech to promote its own political and economic ways of doing things.

ON TOWARD PLANETHOOD

International problems such as air and ocean pollution, disease control, the use of natural resources, and terrorism require international solutions. The world today is one big neighborhood. Two centuries ago, if you got on a stagecoach at 3:00 in the morning and rode until 10:00 that night, you could average 40 miles per day—in good weather! Telephones, radio, and TV have shrunk the globe. Using jet planes you can travel anywhere in hours. With satellite communication today, you can hear and see events all over the world as though they were next door.

> *Science has made unrestricted national sovereignty incompatible with human survival. The only possibilities are now world government or death.*
>
> Bertrand Russell
> Philosopher

Even if humanity's future were not in jeopardy from nuclear weapons, a new world system is essential to the unfolding of a bountiful life for our children. Suppose the United States were broken up into fifty sovereign, separate *national* boundaries. To drive from San Francisco to New York on Interstate Highway 80, (assuming there was an I-80), you'd have to stop and submit to customs and immigration procedures in twelve different countries! And you might have to exchange your money a dozen times to buy things in each separate nation-state. This would enormously reduce the wonderful vitality that the United States has developed as one nation.

When the 159 nations of earth are united into an international system, every aspect of our lives will be greatly enriched—to say nothing of the hundreds of billions of dollars each year that will be transferred from killing machines to more abundant living. We can create a new era with new business opportunities, broader education, increased health care, and greater cultural richness. This is what *PlanetHood* is about.

The eight steps explained in this book give you ways you can help create a world free from war and want. In the First Step, we stressed the importance of asserting our ultimate human right: To live in a peaceful world free from the threat of death from nuclear war. The Second Step requires that we understand what

> *All mankind would be grateful for all time to the statesman who could bring about a new structure of international society.*
>
> Theodore Roosevelt
> Former U.S. President
> Upon accepting the
> Nobel Peace Prize, 1910

needs to be done: Reform the United Nations to complete the world system with international laws, courts, and enforcement—and then safely and permanently disarm all nations.

By thus achieving our planethood, the international "wild west" anarchy will become a colorful historical memory. We will have met the challenge of our time—and won! Our children will have a greater future than any generation that has walked on this earth: freed from the costly arms race, the people of this Earth will enjoy safer and richer lives as we seek our destiny in the Universe.

3rd Step

Become a Peace Patriot

Step 3 will show you how to become a peace patriot. You will actually learn how to follow in George Washington's footsteps and become a modern founder of law and order—throughout the world. Step 3 will add to your insight and motivation to do the job that must be done to save humanity.

In 1776 the American colonies wanted independence from England. Under the leadership of General George Washington, we fought the Revolutionary War, defeated England, and the United States of America was off and running as a great nation. Right? No, wrong!

Except for a few students of history, most people do not realize that after winning the War of Independence from England, there was no government of the United States of America. There were only thirteen sovereign

> The popular notion about the origin of the United States government is that the Declaration of Independence and the United States Constitution were part of a single historical process. There were years of disintegration and deterioration after the end of the Revolution. The United States was not born in 1776 with the Declaration of Independence but in 1787 when the U.S. Constitution came into being.
>
> Norman Cousins
> President, World Federalist Association

nation-states. They got together to draft the "Articles of Confederation and Perpetual Union" to agree on the ground rules for relating to each other.

THE FIRST ATTEMPT

Although completed on November 15, 1777, it took five years for all of the thirteen nation-states to agree to sign the Articles of Confederation and Perpetual Union. Under the Articles, the nation-states agreed not to make alliances, treaties, or set up separate embassies in any foreign nation, not to enter into treaties between themselves without the agreement of the other states, and not to keep any military or naval force except militia needed for internal order. At least nine states had to vote in favor of a major law for it to pass. To make any changes in the Articles, all of the states had to agree unanimously.

> The primary cause of all disorders lies in the different state governments and in the tenacity of that power which pervades the whole of their systems.
>
> George Washington

However, the limited cooperation that existed during the war soon began to evaporate in peacetime. Agreements under the Articles were often ignored when it pleased a state to do so. Under the Articles of Confederation, there was no executive leader, the Continental Congress did not have the power to make enforceable laws, and no court had the power to settle disputes.

There was no way to pay for confederation expenses except by asking the states to contribute their share. Just as the United States and the Soviet Union have done with the United Nations, the nation-states petulantly chose to cut off funds when things didn't go the way they wanted. "By 1786," according to John Fiske in *The Critical Period of American History 1783—1789*, "under the universal depression and want of confidence, all trade had well-nigh stopped, and political quackery, with its cheap and dirty remedies, had full control of the field."

The Articles of Confederation did not base the intended government on the vote of the people. Appointment to the Continental Congress, the funding, and the power came through the thirteen state governments concerned with their private interests. The appointed politicians considered that they represented only the interests of each nation-state. Agreements under the Articles of Confederation were usually ignored. Action in critical matters was blocked by the fear of offending or alienating a state; thus wise overall policies or actions to correct violations of the agreed on Articles were not taken

> We hold these truths to be self-evident, that all men are created equal, that they are endowed by their Creator with certain unalienable Rights, that among these are Life, Liberty and the pursuit of Happiness. That to secure these rights, Governments are instituted among Men, deriving their just powers from the consent of the governed. That whenever any Form of Government becomes destructive of these ends, it is the Right of the People to alter or to abolish it, and to institute new Government, laying its foundation on such principles and organizing its powers in such form, as to them shall seem most likely to effect their Safety and Happiness.
>
> Declaration of Independence, 1776

for "strategic" reasons. The only way to enforce the agreements under the Articles of Confederation was by the threat of war. Doesn't this sound like the U.N. today?

INCREASING CHAOS AND ANARCHY

Since each of the thirteen nation-states could violate without penalty anything they'd agreed to under the Articles, it is not surprising that the United States of America began falling apart. New York funded a lot of its government expenses with tariffs collected on goods from Connecticut and New Jersey—even though such tariffs were forbidden under the Articles. Every "Yankee" ship and New Jersey market boat had to pay entrance fees and clear New York customs just like ships from London or Hamburg. Boycotting the Congress when a state did not get its way was frequent. The Congress often had too few delegates present to do business, it seldom had money in its bank account, and its credit was shot so it could not borrow.

It became obvious that, under the Articles, the states had created only a treaty of alliance and a forum for communicating—not a U.S. Government. Since the Continental Congress was totally without the power to enforce anything, it was in effect simply a "town meeting" of the thirteen sovereign nation-states.

> *There are those who believe that the abolition of war will come only when the hearts of all men are changed to want peace. However, our U.S. government was not formed only after all the people in the thirteen original states had become saints. Instead it was formed to control men of ill will, to set standards by which men could live with one another, encroaching upon each other's freedom as little as possible, and to provide the institutions to settle disputes among states and among people. Our task today is to carry this same concept one level higher, so that a world federation can provide the institutions to settle disputes among nations and among people.*
>
> Tom A. Hudgens
> *Let's Abolish War*

Every year things continued to fly apart. The oyster and crab fishermen of Maryland and Virginia were fighting with one another over fishing rights on the Potomac River. Since Pennsylvania and Delaware also used the Potomac for shipping, they added to the heat of the argument. Under the Articles of Confederation, the Continental Congress was powerless to settle the relatively small issue of the "oyster war."

The peace treaty with England was separately ratified by Virginia in violation of the Articles—as though signing by the Continental Congress was not enough! States had borrowed and were trying to borrow money abroad as if they were separate nations. Nine states from Massachusetts to South Carolina had navies of their own, and all of the states considered their militia as state armies. Under the Articles, Congress had the sole right to provide for coinage, and it had never minted a single U.S. coin! In violation of agreements under the Articles, seven of the states were irresponsibly printing paper money. Since paper money was often worthless, barter was common. Isaiah Thomas, editor of the Worcester *Spy*, announced that you could pay for a subscription to his paper with salt pork.

When Congress in 1781 tried to raise money for its empty treasury by a 5% duty on imported goods, the representatives from New York blocked it because they wanted their own customs system to extract money from the neighboring states. Lacking good ports of its own, New Jersey had to send its exports through New York or Philadelphia and to pay taxes to both of these states. Benjamin Franklin called New Jersey "a keg tapped at both ends."

Things were a mess. In 1785 Connecticut passed a law which gave its manufacturers and merchants an advantage over industries in New York and Massachusetts. As described by Clarence Streit in *Union Now*, "... they lived in a time when New York was protecting its fuel interests by a tariff on Connecticut wood and its farmers by duties on New Jersey butter, when Massachusetts closed while Connecticut opened its ports to British shipping, when Boston was boycotting Rhode Island grain and Philadelphia was refusing to accept New Jersey money, when the money of Connecticut, Delaware and Virginia was sound, that of all other States was variously depreciated and that of Rhode Island and Georgia was so worthless that their governments sought to coerce the citizens into

> *The value of a citizen's currency would shrink 10 percent when he or she crossed a state line. Thus a citizen who started out from New Hampshire with $100 in his pocket would have $20.24 left by the time he arrived in Georgia—without having spent a cent.*
>
> Norman Cousins
> Foreword, *World Federalist Bicentennial Reader*

accepting it. In those days New York was massing troops on its Vermont frontier while the army of Pennsylvania was committing the atrocities of the 'Wyoming massacre' against settlers from Connecticut."

In 1786 many people in the New England states were threatening to leave the Union and start their own confederation.

No wonder that Vernon Nash wrote in *The World Must Be Governed*, "for fatuous proceedings and a low level of snarling debate to match what we have beheld in the Security Council, one must go to the records of the Continental Congress. That body was of no more consequence than the assemblies in each of our modern leagues have been [the League of Nations and the United Nations]. After the Revolutionary War, the Continental Congress suffered the same fate as our two world forums; respect for it, both at home and abroad, declined to the vanishing point."

After four years of turmoil in all parts of the country, with troops called out in several states to handle situations and with civil war narrowly avoided at least half a dozen times, the future looked dark. George Washington was deeply concerned that the United States after winning the war would tear itself apart in peace. He wrote to John Jay in June 1786, "I am uneasy and apprehensive, more so than during the war."

THE CONSTITUTIONAL CONVENTION

Disturbed by festering conflicts, Virginia proposed a meeting in Annapolis in September 1786 to discuss the regulation of trade among the states. The delegates were unable to agree on anything except to meet again in Philadelphia on the second Monday of the following May. This turned out to be the famous Constitutional Convention of 1787. The

> *In the midst of this turmoil, 55 men came together in Philadelphia in the summer of 1787 and drew up a document which provided the framework of government for a nation that became the most successful on earth.*
>
> *The Economist*

Continental Congress authorized it to meet for "the sole purpose of revising the Articles of Confederation, and reporting to Congress and the several Legislatures, such alterations and provisions therein, as shall, when agreed to in Congress, and confirmed by the states, render the Federal Constitution adequate to the exigencies of Government, and the preservation of the Union."

The delegates faced a seemingly impossible task. They were scared of a king getting into power and putting them right back where they were before the War of Independence (just as we are scared stiff of setting up a world government that could be seized by a dictator). The thirteen states were also not willing to give up control of their own affairs. And yet they faced conflict and wars the way things were going. The forms of government that had

> *In 1787 a new nation aborning needed unity more than anything else .... In 1987, it is the whole world that needs to be united.*
> Father Theodore Hesburgh
> Former President, Notre Dame University

been tried in the history of civilization to that date usually erred either on the side of impotency or tyranny. You can choose your poison—there's no way for the people to win. Or so it seemed.

The Founding Fathers of our nation in Philadelphia in the summer of 1787 didn't know how to do it—and yet they knew they had to do it! The biggest problem facing the convention was how to avoid repeating the mistakes of the past. Delegate James Wilson of Pennsylvania observed, "There are two kinds of bad government—the one which does too much and therefore is oppressive, and the other which does too little and therefore is weak." How do you find the fine line between too much power and too little? How do you preserve each state with its individual uniqueness, and yet have an overall power for the common good? How do you balance the rights of minorities and majorities? How do you guarantee individual freedom to the greatest extent consistent with the common good? How do you set things up so fairly that disagreeing people *choose to fight in a court instead of the battlefield?*

They were familiar with the problem of power. The ruthlessness, the ignoring of human rights, the wasting of the people's blood and money on wars had been demonstrated time and time again to be the penalties that are paid for an all-powerful national government that can make and enforce its decisions in a way that is unresponsive to the wishes of the people. And yet the weak government they had set up under the Articles of Confederation was being ignored at will.

Was there any way out of this dilemma? Was it possible to have a government that could avoid falling into the fatal pits of ineffectiveness or of dictatorship? And if such a government could be formed, how would it interact with existing states? If nation-states were to be controlled by a supreme national government, wouldn't this set us up for another war system when states disagreed? The use of military force against a state would be seen as a declaration of war—not as pressure to stop violating an agreement. It would probably be considered by the attacked nation-state as a release from all previous contracts by which it might be bound.

John Fiske clarifies for us the problem of dealing with a nation-state when it breaks the law: "When an individual defies the law, you can lock him up in jail, or levy an execution upon his property. The immense force of the community is arrayed against him, and he is as helpless as a straw on the billows of the ocean. He cannot raise a militia to protect himself. But when the law is defied by a state, it is quite otherwise. You cannot put a state into jail, nor seize its goods; you can only make war on it, and if you try that expedient you find that the state is not helpless. Its local pride and prejudices are aroused against you, and its militia will turn out in full force to uphold the infraction of law."

How can a national government actually support state governments, protect the power of states to make their own decisions about matters within their own state borders, maintain an overall national power with the ability to enforce laws for the good of all the nation-states, and at the same time make everything as responsive as possible to the will of the people? How can you set up an overall government that adds to the *prosperity and protection* of the individual rights of everyone?

> *It was felt by the Statesmen who framed the Constitution, and by the people who adopted it, that it was necessary that many of the rights of sovereignty which the States then possessed should be ceded to the General Government . . . .*
>
> Chief Justice Taney
> U.S. Supreme Court

DIFFICULT ISSUES

When George Washington lowered the gavel on May 25, 1787 at the first session of the Constitutional Convention, many doubted that it could be done because of the fixed instructions the states had given their delegates. For example, the Delaware delegates were prohibited from agreeing to any change in the equal vote of all the states which they enjoyed in the Continental Congress.

The delegates soon realized that the solution to America's problems could not be achieved by revising the Articles. Something more fundamental was needed; a mere patching up would not do the job. It was up to the political geniuses assembled in Philadelphia *to put in place a new system of government* that could steer the ship of state between the shoals of

> ...I have had no wish more ardent, through the whole progress of this business, than that of knowing what kind of government is best calculated for us to live under. No doubt there will be a diversity of sentiments on this important subject; and to inform the judgment, it is necessary to hear all arguments that can be advanced. To please all is impossible and to attempt it would be vain. The only way, therefore ... is, under all the views in which it can be placed, and with due consideration to circumstances, habits, &c., &c., to form such a government as will bear the scrutinizing eye of criticism, and trust it to the good sense and patriotism of the people to carry it into effect. Demagogues, men who are unwilling to lose any of their State consequence, and interested characters in each, will oppose any general government. But let these be regarded rightly, and justice, it is to be hoped, will at length prevail.
> George Washington
> July 1, 1787

ineffectiveness and the reefs of power. Delegate Randolph advised, "When the salvation of the republic is at stake, it would be treason to our trust not to propose what we find necessary."

George Washington knew that the delegates must go beyond their instructions from the states and think afresh to find the answers which would save their dream of a United States. "It is too probable that no plan we propose will be adopted," he told some delegates. "Perhaps another dreadful conflict is to be sustained.

If to please the people, we offer what we ourselves disapprove, how can we afterwards defend our work? Let us raise a standard to which the wise and honest can repair. The event is in the hand of God."

There was disagreement on almost every issue. It took patience and an ability to listen to each other to understand opposing views. The delegates were careful to control their emotions and postponed decisions on touchy issues that would blow the convention apart. They worked day by day, living with disagreement. They were determined to achieve a unified government. *The Great Rehearsal* by Carl Van Doren spells out the fascinating interplay of interests that the Constitutional delegates had to deal with. Van Doren regards the convention as a "great rehearsal" of the process that we need today to create a final layer of world governance that will give humanity a future on this planet.

> *The Federal Convention, viewed from the records, is startlingly fresh and new. The spirit behind it was the spirit of compromise, seemingly no very noble flag to rally round. Compromise can be an ugly word, signifying a pact with the devil, a chipping off of the best to suit the worst. Yet in the Constitutional Convention the spirit of compromise reigned in grace and glory; as Washington presided, it sat on his shoulder like the dove. Men rise to speak and one sees them struggle with the bias of birthright, locality, statehood—South against North, East against West, merchant against planter. One sees them change their minds, fight against pride, and when the moment comes, admit their error.*
>
> Catherine Drinker Bowen
> *Miracle at Philadelphia*

The Convention almost collapsed over the demand of small states to have an equal voice in Congress, and the demand of large states that population be proportionally represented. New York had over 300,000 residents while Delaware had less than 60,000. And Delaware wasn't about to be outvoted!

The solution seems so obvious now with hindsight, but at the time that deadlock had to be met with great creative insight and a willingness to compromise. After all, how could you empower both the large states and the small states simultaneously— and still have an effective government? Roger Sherman of

Connecticut came to the rescue; he suggested that there be two houses of Congress. It was eventually decided that the number of Representatives in the House was to be proportional to each state's population, and the Senate was to have two Senators from each state regardless of size—which makes all states equal. The "impossible" had been accomplished by *compromise*.

COMPROMISE LEADS TO SUCCESS

The delegates were unshakably divided over the issue of slavery and the slave trade from Africa. On August 22 George Mason of Virginia stood up and condemned "the infernal traffic." He later said, "The augmentation of slaves weakens the states; and such a trade is diabolical in itself, and disgraceful to mankind. Yet, by this constitution, it is continued.... As much as I value an union of all the states, I would not admit the Southern states [South Carolina and Georgia] into the union, unless they agree to the discontinuance of this disgraceful trade...." George Washington, Benjamin Franklin, and most delegates from the northern states agreed with him.

Charles Pinckney answered for the other side, "South Carolina can never receive the plan if it prohibits the slave trade." He pointed out that slavery was "justified by the example of all the world." He cited Greece, Rome, and other ancient states; he declared with finality and vehemence that South Carolina and Georgia could not do without slaves.

> *The Constitution that is submitted is not free from imperfections. But there are as few radical defects in it as could well be expected, considering the heterogeneous mass of which the Convention was composed and the diversity of interests that are to be attended to. As a Constitutional door is opened for future amendments and alterations, I think it would be wise in the people to accept what is offered to them.*
>
> George Washington
> On signing the U.S. Constitution

This was a rock-hard, insoluble issue that threatened to destroy the acceptance of the U.S. Constitution by the thirteen nation-states. Should they break up the U.S. into two or even

three different confederations? Or in the interests of achieving
the strength of a common union, should they permit this evil of
the slave trade? Rather than see their dream of a United States
of America condemned to failure because of this or any other
issue, the delegates chose to work out *the best agreements possible*—and leave some problems to be resolved at a later time. As
expressed by John Fiske, they decided that we would have a
"single powerful and pacific federal union instead of being
parcelled out among forty or fifty small communities, wasting
their strength and lowering their moral tone by perpetual warfare . . . . There can be little doubt that slavery and every other
remnant of barbarism in American society would have thriven
far more lustily under a state of chronic anarchy than was
possible under the Constitution."

The issue of slavery was decided over a half-century later
during President Lincoln's administration by an unfortunate
civil war between the southern and northern states. Yet it is likely
that without the com-
promise that let our
U.S. federal govern-
ment be formed, *the
bloodshed over this
issue and many other
issues* between thir-
teen proud, assertive
nation-states would
have brought about

> *The intolerable anarchy which was
> swiftly created by the exercise of autono-
> mous sovereignty by the thirteen states
> over matters of common concern drove our
> forefathers into union. Most of them took
> every step in that direction with misgivings,
> with reluctance, and often with repug-
> nance.*
>
> Vernon Nash
> *The World Must Be Governed*

enormously more suffering and death over the years *for both
blacks and whites.* The founders of our nation *did not want to
lose all* by holding out for everything they individually wanted.

It is easy to tighten a disagreement so that it becomes
absolutely nonnegotiable—and it can feel good to pound the
table with indignation and righteousness. When we do this, our
ability to work together for our mutual good can be destroyed.
Many people feel today that no issue should be permitted to stand
in the way of creating a worldwide federation that can save

humanity from nuclear holocaust. Once we achieve such a world governance, we will have a fine vehicle for protecting human rights without bloodying up the planet.

FINISHING THE JOB

So day after day through the long hot summer, the delegates continued their difficult work, trying to find the wavering line between too much and too little. They worked out agreements on how to enact taxes, appropriate money, and approve foreign treaties. They limited the power of all three branches of the overall government by ingenious checks and balances. Since there was no chief executive under the Articles of Confederation, they

> *The Constitution which we now present is the result of a spirit of amity and of the mutual deference and concession which the peculiarity of our political situation rendered indispensable.*
>
> George Washington
> On submitting the Constitution
> to the Continental Congress

carefully laid out the limited powers of the President. The functions of the Senate, House of Representatives, and Supreme Court were likewise specified. The Constitution was to go into effect when nine states ratified it. These and other details of this superb political invention were finally summed up in seven articles.

The finished product was not thoroughly satisfying to anyone at the convention. Benjamin Franklin who was internationally viewed as one of the wisest philosophers and greatest scientists of the age, expressed the attitude of most of the delegates to the Constitutional Convention: "I confess that there are several parts of this constitution which I do not at present approve . . . ." Franklin was a master at helping people go from conflict to unity:

But I am not sure I shall never approve them. For having lived long, I have experienced many instances of being obliged by better information or fuller consideration, to change opinions even on important subjects, which I once thought right, but found to be otherwise. It is therefore that the older I grow, the more apt I am to doubt my own judgment, and to pay more respect to the judgment of others. Most men indeed as well as most sects in religion, think themselves in possession of all truth, and that wherever others differ from them it is so far error . . . . But though many private persons think almost as highly of their own infallibility as that of their sect, few express it so naturally as a certain French lady, who in a dispute with her sister, said, "I don't know how it happens, Sister, but I meet with nobody but myself, that's always in the right"—*Il n'y a que moi qui a toujours raison.* In these sentiments, Sir, I agree to this Constitution with all its faults, if they are such . . . .

Franklin eloquently summed it up, "I consent, Sir, to this Constitution, because I expect no better and because I am not sure that it is not the best. The opinions I have had of its errors, I sacrifice to the public good . . . ."

The hesitation of our politicians today to lead us by supporting a binding world system of law and order is understandable. Carl Van Doren tells us, "Not one of the delegates about to sign could feel certain that their plan would be accepted by the state conventions or ever go into effect. They might have wasted all their time and effort. They might by their proposals have raised up political enmities which would put an end to their own public careers. They could not foresee that to have signed the Constitution would in the future make them all remembered, however little else they might have done—as the Founding Fathers of their country."

On that great Monday, September 17, the Constitution of the United States of America was signed by every state delegation present. Of those present, only Governor Randolph and Colonel Mason from Virginia, and Elbridge Gerry from Massachusetts individually refused to sign. It is warming to note that Gerry would later become a representative to the first Congress of the new nation and Vice President under Madison, and that Randolph would be the Attorney General and Secretary of State under Washington.

APPROVAL BY THE PEOPLE

The Philadelphia convention sent its proposed constitution to the Continental Congress in New York, which sent it to the state legislatures. The state legislatures called for state conventions that would decide if the people were in favor of this new vehicle for governing themselves.

Patrick Henry didn't like it. (You'll recall he roused people in the spirit of '76 with his famous "Give me liberty or give me death.") He predicted that state established religion would be set up under the new Constitution, and Kentuckians would lose the right to navigate the Mississippi River. Mason attacked the character of the Constitutional delegates, calling them "Knaves and Fools," "a parcel of Coxcombs," and "Office Hunters not a few."

> *Whilst the last members were signing it, Doctr. Franklin looking towards the Presidents chair, at the back of which a rising sun happened to be painted, observed to a few members near him, that Painters had found it difficult to distinguish in their art a rising from a setting sun. I have, said he, ... often in the course of the Session, and the vicissitudes of my hopes and fears as to its issue, looked at that behind the President without being able to tell whether it was rising or setting: But now at length I have the happiness to know that it is a rising and not a setting Sun.*
>
> James Madison, September 1787
> Delegate, Constitutional Convention

George Washington in a letter to Lafayette on February 7, 1788 said, "It appears to me, then, little short of a miracle, that the Delegates from so many different states (which states you know are also different from each other), in their manners, circumstances, and prejudices, should unite in forming a system of national government . . . ." Supporters for the new federal constitution had an uphill battle. One future president, Monroe, and the fathers of two future presidents, Harrison and Tyler, were anti-federalists who fought against ratification.

The signers of the Constitution did not abandon their baby, but worked diligently at the state level to secure ratification. Hamilton and Madison (with some help from John Jay) published a series of 85 essays entitled *The Federalist*. All were signed "Publius." These were picked up by the newspapers and the issues were strenuously debated by the people as the big controversy of the day.

While working for ratification, Hamilton responded to the accusation that he was too cynical when he said that the solemn pledges of nations are untrustworthy. Hamilton retorted, "Do we depend for the maintenance of domestic order upon the mere promises of individuals to behave themselves?" Then he profoundly posed:

> Why has government been instituted at all? Because the passions of men will not conform to the dictates of reason and justice without restraint. Has it been found that bodies of men act with more rectitude and greater disinterestedness than individuals? The contrary of this has been inferred by all accurate observers of the conduct of mankind.

Before meeting in Philadelphia, Delaware had instructed its delegates not to have anything to do with a constitution that did not give it an equal vote with all other states. On December 7, 1787, Delaware was the first to ratify—quickly and without a single dissenting vote! When the Pennsylvania state convention was meeting to consider ratification, it received the news that Delaware had ratified. One of the delegates, Smilie, sourly commented that Delaware had "reaped the honor of having first surrendered the liberties of the people." The majority of the delegates, however, felt that Pennsylvania's liberty and future prosperity would be better protected by being part of the federal union. They voted to ratify the constitution only four days after Delaware ratified!

This was followed by New Jersey, Georgia, Connecticut, Massachusetts, Maryland, and South Carolina. New Hampshire on June 21, 1788 was the ninth state to ratify, and thereby completed the number needed for the new federal government to go into effect. Just four days later Virginia ratified by a

> *The moment this plan goes forth, all other considerations will be laid aside— and the greatest question will be, shall there be a national government or not? And this must take place or a general anarchy will be the alternative.*
> Gouverneur Morris, 1787
> Delegate, Constitutional Convention

10-vote majority, and New York by only 3 votes. North Carolina on August 2, 1788, declined to act on the new constitution but changed its mind a year and a half later. It joined the Union on November 21, 1789.

Rhode Island had been torn in a conflict between the townspeople and farmers. It had not even sent delegates to the Constitutional Convention in 1787. After the federal government had been in operation for two years, the Senate told the state that it was severing commercial relations between the United States and Rhode Island. Rhode Island finally realized that it could not provide itself with the security and prosperity that would be possible for its citizens if it joined the federal union. By a margin of only two votes, three years after the Constitutional Convention, on May 29, 1790 it ratified the Constitution of the United States. Now all thirteen of the original nation-states had come together in creating a federal government that permitted the greatness of all the individual states to unfold! At the urging of the citizens of various states, the first ten amendments to the U.S. Constitution (the Bill of Rights) were quickly ratified.

OUR WAY IS CLEAR

"In 1787," Carl Van Doren explains in *The Great Rehearsal*, "the problem was how the people could learn to think nationally, not locally, about the United States." The problem today is how the people can learn to *think internationally, not nationally, about the world.* Surely, there will be opposition to the idea. Some may call it naive, idealistic, or premature. These were the same attitudes which our Founding Fathers overcame—and so can we.

There are some who argue that creating a world congress, courts, and executive branch is much more difficult today than it was in the simpler world of our forefathers two hundred years ago. That may be true, but we should not forget that our technical means of communication and the ability to solve complex problems is now infinitely greater. The compelling urgency of the need should provide the extra inspiration and determination to overcome the obstacles.

The challenges that faced America back then must have seemed as great to them as ours do to us. Patriot Tom Paine noted that the thirteen colonies were "made up of people from different nations, accustomed to different forms and habits of government, speaking different languages, and more different in their models of worship." Pennsylvania and Delaware had religious freedom for Christians, in Rhode Island Catholics could not vote, and in Massachusetts, Catholic priests were liable to imprisonment for life! They had no common currency or system of taxation, and there were trade and travel restrictions between the states. They were divided into liberals and conservatives. Some depended upon slavery for their existence, and others regarded it as an abomination. It was North vs. South, East vs. West, planter vs. merchant, and one religion against another. Some of the states were talking about war with each other!

> *There were times in the Convention of 1787 when it seemed that the requirements of the individual states in their nationalistic American world were insurmountable. But the American Constitution has proved that none of the American "nations" actually had interests that were more vital to them than were the interests of America as a whole.*
>
> Lloyd Graham
> *The Desperate People*

Yet with all this diversity, two centuries ago the patriots put the Constitution together in about 100 working days (May 25 to September 17). From conception on September 17, 1787 to official birth on June 21, 1788, our federal republic only took nine months! And in those days it took three weeks to travel from Philadelphia to Atlanta! And no telephones, either!

THE FEDERAL SOLUTION

The Founding Fathers accomplished this great union by designing a government that *honored and included* the thirteen separate nation-states instead of putting itself in opposition to them as unruly delinquents to be punished when they got out of line. They did this by leaving each nation-state in control of almost all of the decisions that af-

> *The federal idea, which our Founding Fathers applied in their historical act of political creation in the eighteenth century, can be applied in this twentieth century in the larger context of the world of free nations—if we will but match our forefathers in courage and vision.*
>
> Nelson A. Rockefeller
> *The Future of Federalism*
> Harvard University Press

fect its own citizens. Since the people of each state had their own state legislatures, it was up to the voters to make sure they were getting the state government they wanted. Then by creating an added layer of Federal government that would handle national problems that could not be solved by individual states, they minimized the risk of interstate conflict. The national government could make and enforce decisions that required states to cooperate with each other and to support activities that served the common good.

This is the next step we must accomplish for the world to survive the international anarchy and lawlessness of today. This political invention has been tested by the U.S. for over 200 years—and it has been copied by dozens of other nations throughout the world.

TO SUM UP

In our own way, *we must adapt* this basic political invention to the world of today. To do this you will need to take Step 4 (explained in the next chapter) that tells about the enormous progress we've made in the last forty years toward world law, courts, and enforcement. We can be optimistic about achieving our ultimate right to live in a peaceful world

> *There is one thing stronger than all the armies of the world and that is an idea whose time has come.*
>
> Victor Hugo

free from the threat of death by nuclear war. We're not starting at the bottom of the ladder—in fact we're nearly at the top!!! We expect that you will be amazed by our progress so far—and deeply inspired to help the world complete the final layer of government on which our common survival depends.

You'll recall the story of patriot Paul Revere who galloped across the countryside to warn people of the approach of the English troops: "The Redcoats are coming!" Will you appoint yourself as a nuclear age Paul Revere? Will you make sure that your neighbors are awakening to the greatest danger humanity has ever faced? And will you tell them the great news of how we can reform the United Nations and take the other necessary steps to save ourselves and our children—and give the world more security and a richer life than ever before?

As modern Paul Reveres, let's not stop until the job is done.

4th Step

Recognize Our Great Progress

More progress has been made in *international law* in the past forty years than in previous thousands. We must escape from being discouraged by judgments of "too idealistic," "utopian," or "not practical." If we peer into the past, we will better appreciate the present. In the evolution of law, courts, and enforcement—the essential building blocks for a peaceful world—the perspective of history reveals *an almost incredible record of recent accomplishment.* The world has been getting ready for a great transformation! In fact, it has already begun.

THE GROWTH OF INTERNATIONAL LAW

It took thousands of years to move from the primitive law of the pre-Christian era to the beginnings of international law. We are indebted to the swashbuckling pirates for the first clear beginnings of international criminal law. As they plundered ships on the high seas, they obviously were not subject to the territorial laws of any one country. Since they threatened the free flow of commerce, something had to be done. By common understanding of maritime nations, they were outlawed as "the enemies of all mankind" and tried and punished wherever and whenever they might be captured. *Separate nations were able to cooperate to solve a common problem.* Because of this, piracy is no longer a serious concern.

One of the early founders of international law was Franciscus de Victoria, a Spaniard who studied at the Sorbonne in Paris before being appointed Primary Professor of Sacred Theology at

> *It is obvious that no difficulty in the way of a world government can match the danger of a world without it.*
>
> Carl van Doren
> *The Great Rehearsal*

the University of Salamanca in 1526. He taught that all wars have to be morally justifiable—to right a wrong. According to Victoria, differences of religion or the personal glory of a king were not acceptable reasons for killing people of other nations. He said that no subject was bound to serve in an unjust war even if commanded by his king. This bad news for the tyrants could only be published 150 years after Victoria's death. It was assembled from his students' lecture notes. Victoria is recognized as one of the pioneers of international law. His statue stands in the garden outside the United Nations today.

The person universally acclaimed as the father of international law is the great Dutch jurist Hugo Grotius. In 1625 he completed his famous three books on the *Laws of War and Peace*. Grotius listed three methods to prevent violence between nations: (1) conferences, (2) arbitration, or (3) by lot as had been suggested by Solomon. As a much lesser evil than a killing war between armies, he explained that the kings and tyrants might settle their differences by single combat between themselves—an idea that the U.N. seems to have overlooked! He urged that we have humane conduct even in war, "Lest by imitating wild beasts too much we forget to be human."

The first chair for the teaching of "the law of nations" was established at the University of Heidelberg and Samuel Pufendorf was its first professor. He published *On the Law of Nature and Nations* in 1688. Even at the time of the Constitutional Convention in Philadelphia, the expression "international law" was still virtually unknown. This term had been introduced only several years earlier by Jeremy Bentham when he published *Principles of International Law* in 1783.

David Dudley Field was among the notables who contributed to a flood of ideas in international law. He had codified the laws of the State of New York and was the first President of the unofficial International Law Association. In 1872 he drafted *Outlines of an International Code* which called for arbitration of disputes and collective enforcement actions. Professor Pasquale Fiore of Italy in 1880 for the first time referred to the "scourge of war" as the "greatest of all crimes." *The seeds of international law were sprouting and taking root.*

IN THE TWENTIETH CENTURY

In an attempt to relieve the very heavy burden of the arms race, in 1899 Nicholas II, the Czar of Russia, proposed that the "civilized states" meet at The Hague for what was heralded as the first "international peace conference." It was attended by 26 nations. In the second Hague conference in 1907, the number of participants increased to 44—a measure of progress. Unfortunately, they largely dealt with international rules for military combat, as they were unwilling to genuinely give up their age-old privilege of settling disputes by killing people in other nations. Instead of laying down binding rules for peace, all that the self-styled "civilized states" could do was to agree upon rules for waging war!

> *The real cause of all wars has always been the same . . . . Wars between groups of men forming social units always take place when these units—tribes, dynasties, churches, cities, nations—exercise unrestricted sovereign power. Wars between these social units cease the moment sovereign power is transferred from them to a larger or higher unit . . . . The question is not one of 'surrendering' national sovereignty. The problem is not negative and does not involve giving up something we already have. The problem is positive—creating something we lack . . . but imperatively need . . . the extension of law and order into another field of human association which heretofore has remained unregulated and in anarchy.*
>
> Emery Reves
> *The Anatomy of Peace*

It took World War I, with 20 million people killed, before nations began to realize that the prevailing international system was in need of revision. All people everywhere yearned for a more secure and peaceful world. President Woodrow Wilson played a leading role in establishing the League of Nations as "a general association of nations" to protect "great and small states alike." *The 1919 Covenant for a League of Nations, based upon ideas that had been evolving for centuries, envisaged codification of international law, a court to settle disputes, arms control, collective security, and social justice.* It was a great milestone in the zig-zagging line of progress toward a world government. But a handful of isolationist Senators headed by Henry Cabot Lodge blocked American membership in the League of Nations. The nation that had conceived the infant abandoned its own child. The U.S. never joined. *It was not the League that failed the nations; the nations failed the League.* Thus the door was opened to the even greater tragedy of World War II.

> *There can be no peace without law.*
> Dwight D. Eisenhower
> October 31, 1956
> Former U.S. President

ANOTHER STEP FORWARD

After World War II, international law took a great leap ahead. In 1945, the United States again took the lead in proposing an improved system of international law and order. The goal expressed in the Charter of the United Nations was "to maintain international peace and security . . . in conformity with the principles of justice and international law."

With a new fervor, special U.N. committees were assigned to codify the law of nations. Within the next few decades, aggression, genocide, and crimes against humanity were unanimously condemned as criminal acts. Declarations spelled out the civil, political, economic, social, and cultural rights of all peoples. International accords opened the door to freedom from colonialism.

Inspired by the U.N., nations agreed on "Principles of International Law Governing Friendly Relations Among States." Apartheid was declared an international crime. Aggression was defined by consensus. The Helsinki Agreement sought to assure "Security and Cooperation in Europe." Conventions outlawed torture, the taking of hostages, and other acts of terrorism. Work was begun on a comprehensive code of offenses against the

> *What has resulted [in the U.N. Charter] is a human document with human imperfections but with human hopes and human victory as well. But whatever its imperfections, the Charter ... offers the world an instrument by which a real beginning may be made upon the work of peace.*
>
> Report of the U.S. Secretary of State
> to the President, 1945

peace and security of mankind. A monumental Law of the Sea was accepted by many nations. Multinational treaties were signed in great profusion.

Admittedly, key provisions were often left deliberately vague and open to conflicting interpretations. But that should come as no surprise. *Nations were just beginning to learn that the sovereignty of the state must yield to the sovereignty of the law.* The U.N. Charter was another important step forward, but we were not there yet. It was deliberately put together with nonbinding loopholes that made it unable to preserve peace. There have been about 130 wars since 1945 with an estimated 16 million dead in which the Security Council did not use the power given it in the Charter to stop the aggression and killing.

INTERNATIONAL COURTS BEGIN

We've now looked at the first great steps in which humankind attempted to create lasting peace through international global cooperation: the League of Nations and the United Nations. Now let's examine the great progress we've made in this century in the evolution of international courts. Just as the growth of law from earliest times was a slow and difficult *but continually accelerating process*, history reveals a similar

82

evolutionary pattern regarding the courts needed to settle disputes by peaceful means.

The Hague meetings at the turn of the century recognized the need for a system to settle disputes peacefully, but all they could agree upon at that time was a weak procedure for arbitration.

On the American continent, a Central American Court of Justice was created in 1908 as part of a peace treaty signed by several Central American republics. The national legislators of five participating states elected the five judges. Each nation let go of some of its sovereignty when it agreed to be bound by the decision of the Court. The agreements creating this court were scheduled to expire in ten years. Between 1908 and 1918, ten cases came before it. One of its decrees (involving a complaint by Honduras) that Guatemala and El Salvador were supporting a revolution against Honduras may have prevented a new Central American war. *Despite its limited period of life, the Central American Court of Justice was the first international tribunal of its kind in history.*

> *World federation is an idea that will not die. More and more people are coming to realize that peace must be more than an interlude if we are to survive; that peace is a product of law and order; that law is essential if the force of arms is not to rule the world.*
>
> William O. Douglas
> Former U.S. Supreme Court Justice

Following World War I, a stronger *Permanent Court of International Justice* was established at The Hague. But nations were not yet ready to accept the recommendations of legal experts. The new institution, commonly known as the *World Court*, was only authorized to settle disputes "which the parties thereto shall submit to it." Would you feel safe if a murderer in your town could only be tried by a court if the alleged killer agrees to it?

Even with this serious shortcoming, the *Permanent Court* was an improvement over what had existed before. In the brief period between world wars, its opinions helped to clarify and develop international law. After 1945, it was renamed *The*

International Court of Justice, its procedures were improved, and its work now continues under the U.N. Charter. It is staffed by fifteen outstanding judges from various nations.

After World War II—*for the first time*—temporary international criminal tribunals were established at Nuremberg, Tokyo, and elsewhere to try German and Japanese war criminals for crimes against peace, war crimes, and crimes against humanity.

PERMANENT INTERNATIONAL COURTS

Many permanent multinational courts have been established. The best example is the *Court of Justice of the European Community*. This Court has compulsory jurisdiction to settle disputes that arise under treaties which established the Common Market and the European Atomic Energy Community. *It has settled thousands of commercial disputes which in the past frequently led to military conflicts.* Now nearly a dozen European nations use international law instead of armies to settle such disagreements!

The *European Court of Human Rights* at Strasbourg protects individual rights in western Europe. "Most citizens of the member states of the Council of Europe (21 at present)," according to Ferdinand Kinksy, "have their human rights not only guaranteed by their own national constitution, but also by the European convention for human rights. Should their

> *One should not forget the capacities of the International Court .... The General Assembly and the Security Council could approach it more often for consultative conclusions on international disputes. Its mandatory jurisdiction should be recognized by all on mutually agreed upon conditions.*
>
> Mikhail Gorbachev
> Soviet General Secretary
> Article in *Pravda*, September 17, 1987

national government violate their human rights, European citizens have the possibility to go to a European court, whose judgment has to be respected by the individual states. The member states of the European communities (the twelve common market countries) did transfer part of their sovereignty to the community's institutions. Of course, these 'pre-federalist' elements are not sufficient to make a true federation of the European Community. Neither foreign nor security policies are covered by the EEC treaties." But a new European Parliament is beginning to deal with problems with political consequences.

A new *Inter-American Court of Human Rights* in Costa Rica is beginning to follow a pattern similar to the European court. International agencies, dealing with such areas as banking, health, labor, trade, and atomic energy have developed legal procedures for settling disputes. New administrative tribunals of all kinds have begun to flourish. Today proposals are being considered for an international court to resolve conflicts relating to outer space and environmental problems.

The Law of the Sea Treaty requires almost all disputes to be settled by an International Tribunal. It is in the process of being ratified by various nations. A proposed *International Criminal Court* to deal with international terrorism was endorsed by the American Bar Association in 1978. As a neutral forum, it could avoid today's problems in extraditing terrorists who take advantage of national boundary lines to escape justice.

The Soviet Union is also moving toward the position taken by the American Bar Association. In an article published on September 17, 1987, General Secretary Gorbachev wrote: "A drastic intensification and expansion of cooperation between states in uprooting international terrorism is extremely important. It would be expedient to concentrate this cooperation within the framework of the United Nations organization. In our opinion, it would be useful to create under its aegis a tribunal to investigate acts of international terrorism . . . ."

> We must establish a rule of law, a world rule of law. We have to realize that the world needs policemen who serve the interests of all mankind.
>
> Ramsey Clark
> Former U.S. Attorney General

Despite the hesitation of some important countries, the record shows that nations are gradually becoming accustomed to letting go of enough sovereignty to settle disputes in international courts instead of on the battlefield. War and killing are damaging and expensive; doing combat in international courts is a real bargain by comparison! Humanity can no longer afford to pay the price of the costly method of going to war.

REGIONAL COOPERATION INCREASES

Regional thinking and organization have today become a fact of life all over the globe. Despite centuries of feuds, linguistic differences, and cultural barriers, the west European states have formed a European Community and elected a European Parliament. These rival countries that had suffered the horrible ravages of centuries of war were determined to begin trading, working, and living together in peaceful community.

As smaller nations have come to recognize their need for more security, they have increasingly joined in new cooperative associations and coalitions to enhance their economic, religious, political, or other interests. An Organization of American States has been formed. An Organization of African Unity has come into existence. A League

> *The international community should support a system of laws to regularize international relations and maintain the peace in the same manner that law governs national order.*
>
> Pope John Paul II

of Arab States has been created. Nordic states have joined together for expanded coalition. Southeast Asian Nations have formed a similar coalition for the Pacific. Developing countries have formed a "Group of 77." Over a hundred nations have belied their "non-aligned" status by aligning themselves to further their common interests.

A host of international organizations and specialized agencies, both governmental and nongovernmental, have taken steps toward planethood in hundreds of ways that were inconceivable not long ago. A few of the better known organizations include the International Atomic Energy Agency, the International Maritime Organization, the International Civil Aviation

Organization, a World Meteorological Organization, as well as many agencies dealing with health, commerce, finance, trade, and development. *Within recent memory, the land, the seas, and the skies have become areas of increasing international cooperation.*

ENFORCING INTERNATIONAL LAW

Now let's turn our attention to the steps we've taken toward enforcing international law. We'll find an emerging pattern of gradual progress. The Covenant of the League of Nations and the U.N. Charter both provided for enforcement by economic sanctions, control of armaments, and an international army—but the plans have never been put into effect because the major powers have failed to live up to their obligations.

However, in 1950 in Korea, an international military force under U.N. command was sent into action to halt aggression. This was "the first effort to enforce the principles of collective security through a worldwide international organization." When war erupted in the Congo in 1960, a U.N. military force was authorized to restore law and order, and to expel foreign troops from the newly independent country. For over 20 years, U.N. Peacekeeping Forces have been deployed in Cyprus to prevent war between Turkish and Greek nationalists.

> *The only security for Americans today, or for any people, is in the creation of a system of world order that enables nations to retain sovereignty over their own cultures and institutions but that creates a workable authority for regulating the behavior of nations in their relationships with one another.*
>
> Norman Cousins
> President, World Federalist Association

In the Middle-East, when Egypt nationalized the Suez Canal in 1956, Israel, France, and England invaded the country to protect their interests. The Security Council was powerless because of the British and French veto. But the Soviet Union and the United States arranged for an Emergency Session of the

General Assembly. *Even though it had no Charter authority, the Assembly voted to establish an international force to halt the hostilities.* A U.N. Emergency Force from ten nations was quickly assembled. The invaders cleared out in a hurry!

In 1967, a unanimous decision of the Security Council de-

> *If the rule of law is to govern the community of states and protect it against violations of the international public order, it can only be satisfactorily established by the promulgation of an international penal code and by the permanent functioning of an international criminal jurisdiction.*
>
> Richard Alfaro, 1950
> Former President of Panama

manded a cease-fire and ended the fighting between Egypt and Israel within six days. In 1973, an agreement between U.S. Secretary of State Kissinger and Soviet Chairman Brezhnev brought the "Day of Atonement" war to an abrupt halt. When the superpowers were united, peace became enforceable.

United Nations forces, relying more on armbands than on arms, are playing an increasingly useful role in separating antagonists and monitoring borders in many regions. They can do much more for peace if they are strengthened, supported, and given a fair chance.

PROGRESS IN SOCIAL JUSTICE

International concern for human rights and welfare is a great historical force of our time. One can hardly imagine the chaos and increased suffering that would exist in the world today were it not for cooperative actions taken during the past few decades by U.N. organizations.

The World Health Organization, for example, has totally eradicated smallpox from the face of the earth, and all but eliminated malaria. The Food and Agriculture Organization has "freedom from hunger" as its goal. U.N. programs deal with housing, the rights of women and children, the physically handicapped, refugees, the illiterate, the uneducated, and the disadvantaged in many fields. Economic aid to underdeveloped countries has become a primary world concern.

It was Ambassador Arvid Pardo, of the tiny island of Malta, who gave expression to the inspiring dream that the vast resources of the ocean were "the common heritage of mankind." That humanitarian principle is slowly moving toward reality today. It was confirmed in a 1967 treaty governing the moon and outer space and a 1980 treaty covering the vast continent of Antarctica. Most nations are beginning to accept the idea that all of humankind should somehow share the untapped wealth of our planet.

> *Needed changes will only come about as the expression of the political will of peoples in many parts of the world.*
> Olaf Palme, 1982
> Former Prime Minister of Sweden
> Chairman of the Independent Commission on Disarmament and Security

In the short space of one lifetime—hardly a blink in the eye of time—there has been an awakening of the human conscience. Human rights are now monitored and protected by many governments and organizations around the world. *We are slowly edging in the direction of an international cooperation only previously dreamed of.*

PROGRESS TOWARD DISARMAMENT

The problem of disarmament is the heart of the most vital challenge to the international order. Both the Covenant of the League of Nations and the U.N. Charter called for reductions of national arms. The wisdom of the plan was recognized, even though states were not yet ready to implement it. In the intervening years, however, slow and steady progress has been made.

In 1959, Soviet Premier Nikita Khruschev, speaking at the United Nations, called for general and complete disarmament. In 1961 President John F. Kennedy appointed John J. McCloy, a former Assistant Secretary of War and a distinguished public servant, to serve as his Special Assistant for Disarmament, and to seek an agreement with the Russians.

In September of that year, McCloy and Deputy Soviet Foreign Minister Zorin drew up a joint statement of principles in which both sides recognized that general and complete disarmament was the goal of both nations. They agreed that disarmament was to take place under *"strict and effective international controls."* New institutions would be created to settle disputes by peaceful means. An international peace force would replace national armed forces, which would be disbanded. The intelligent, concise McCloy-Zorin plan was promptly hailed by the entire General Assembly of the United Nations.

President Kennedy challenged the Soviet Union not to an arms race but a peace race "to advance together step by step, stage by stage, until general and complete disarmament has actually been achieved." The heads of state of the two superpowers publicly

> *What is called for is total disarmament—universal, enforceable and complete.*
>
> John J. McCloy, 1959
> Former U.S. Asst. Secretary of War

declared before the whole world that they both favored general and complete disarmament. Unfortunately, suspicion and fear of change continued to paralyze both nations.

Although the excellent McCloy-Zorin plan for general and complete disarmament was never implemented, *it showed how much many people in the U.S., the U.S.S.R., and throughout the globe* want to secure the ultimate human right to live in a peaceful world free from the threat of death by nuclear war. In reaching agreement in December 1987 on the elimination of all intermediate-range nuclear weapons, the two superpowers overcame the problem of verification which had stymied implementation of the McCloy-Zorin principles.

The door of opportunity has now been opened. Let general disarmament and peace walk in. Let us find security not in instruments of death, but through an improved international system based on laws, courts, and effective enforcement.

OUR CONTINUING PROGRESS

Nuclear-free zones have already been created by common consent in many areas of the world including outer space and the moon. Some limits have been placed on nuclear weapons tests. There are agreements to cope with nuclear accidents, and "hot-lines" have been introduced to reduce the risks of miscalculation.

The Anti-Ballistic Missile Treaty of 1972 (ABM) which was ratified as part of SALT I constituted a major step forward. Restraints on nuclear proliferation have been accepted. SALT II (Strategic Arms Limitations Talks)—even though not ratified by the United States—has generally been honored by both sides.

Thirty-five nations meeting recently at the Stockholm Conference on Security in Europe agreed to notify each other of military maneuvers and to allow on-site inspections. It was, according to the West German Ambassador "a victory of reason, responsibility and realism." The Forty-nation Committee on Disarmament, after 18 years of effort, announced on April 29, 1987, that a pact banning all chemical weapons was expected early in 1988. It was announced that the U.S. and U.S.S.R. had agreed on a joint exploration of the Cosmos. A Treaty on the Non-Use of Force that had been debated at the U.N. for many years was adopted by consensus at the end of 1987. It had its loopholes but was nonetheless a significant step forward.

> *I do feel that some minimum of global government to abolish war, to cope with pollution, is absolutely necessary.*
> Arnold Toynbee
> Noted Historian

Some ice was broken in Iceland when President Reagan and Soviet General Secretary Gorbachev met at Reykjavik in October 1986. The summit meeting demonstrated how close the two leaders could come to major arms accords—and how they were able to agree on common goals.

On the difficult problem of verification, former Presidents Gerald Ford and Jimmy Carter, following an unofficial conference with Soviet experts in the spring of 1985, confirmed that past agreements had basically been followed. *Carter was convinced "that even the more contentious issues could be resolved by the superpowers in a mutually satisfactory way."* President Reagan's Commission on Strategic Forces (which employed the services of two former National Security Advisors, four former Secretaries of Defense, three former CIA Directors, and two former Secretaries of State) concluded that *the goal of an effective verification system "remains within our reach."* Indeed, an effective agreement on verification *was* reached in December 1987.

The INF Treaty signed by Reagan and Gorbachev in December 1987 provides for the elimination of all intermediate-range nuclear missiles. Other nuclear arms reductions are being discussed. We hope this and other steps toward disarmament can be implemented. *However it will be mostly window-dressing to look good to the public (and hopefully save some money) until decision-makers and their supporters are willing to take a chance for peace through world law, courts, and enforcement.*

Reduction of nuclear missiles is only a beginning. **Conventional arms today are enormously more effective at killing than the equipment used in World War II.** Chemical warfare and other scientific developments can equal nuclear weapons in their ability to destroy life on this planet. Planethood requires us to remove all arms from the control of individual nations (except for domestic needs). Only then, with international Peacekeeping Forces, will we have the peace and security that we had hoped to achieve through armaments.

> *The dogmas of the quiet past are inadequate to the stormy present. We must think anew and act anew.*
>
> Abraham Lincoln

ON TOWARD SUCCESS

Six tapestries adorn the halls of the U.N. Palace in Geneva, (the original Peace Palace for the League of Nations). They tell the story of our aspirations and progress toward an improved structure of international society. The artists depict the evolution of social life from the family to the clan, the village, the feudal estate, the national state, and—finally—to an international system of government in which people of all races are joined together in a circle of peace. In the course of some six thousand years of recorded history, humankind has been slowly moving toward that sublime ideal. We're almost there!

It took the American Revolution to create the chaos that led to the birth of the Federal Constitution. It took World War I with 20 million dead to inspire statesmen to bring forth a League of Nations. It took World War II with 35 million killed to induce the nation-states to create the United Nations. Each was a great step forward.

The Soviet Union is now calling for a new Comprehensive System of International Peace and Security. On September 17, 1987 Gorbachev in *Pravda* acknowledged that our diverse world is interlinked and interdependent. He called for international cooperation in all fields: military, political, economic, ecological, and humanitarian. He stated that disarmament is a desired goal, including the elimination of all foreign bases and the recall of Soviet troops from Afghanistan. He advocated respect for the U.N. Charter and stronger monitoring to avert wars. He called for international verification of arms limitation treaties (as the U.S. has demanded). He reaffirmed the right to live in dignity, and the importance of international law and order. He even referred to binding jurisdiction being given to the International Court of Justice.

> *Only the unity of all can bring the well-being of all.*
>
> Robert Muller
> Former U.N. Assistant Secy.-Gen.
> Chancellor, World Peace Univ.
> *A Planet of Hope*

This plan was presented to the United Nations. Said Mr. Gorbachev, "The imperatives of the moment call on us to raise many of the principles of everyday common sense to the level of policy." Finding the world threatened with destruction, the

Soviet leader put his finger on the main point: "Nothing will change unless we start to act."

The goals advocated by the Soviet leader in his new policy of openness are goals which the United States has always cherished. If the U.S. is to remain a world leader, it must not hesitate to lead. If the leaders won't lead, let the people lead—and the "leaders" will have to follow. It's up to us!

> *I am strongly convinced that the best method of ultimately securing disarmament is the establishment of an international court and the development of a code of international equity which nations will recognize as affording a better method of settling international controversies than war.*
>
> Howard Taft, 1910
> Former U.S. President

Because of the great progress we have made in developing and using international law in the 20th Century, we are now ready to take the final step toward planethood. We can be inspired by the progress we have made, step by step, decade by decade, toward international law, international courts of justice, and international enforcement.

The 21st Century draws near. We've been window shopping long enough. Now it's time to buy! Step Five tells us how to do this by updating our vehicle for survival and prosperity. Victory lies before us!

5th
Step

Make the U.N.
Effective
for the
Nuclear
Age

Since the end of World War II, our failure to create an effective world system to maintain the peace has resulted in millions killed, many more injured, businesses disrupted, lives twisted through fear and hatred, property destroyed, and enormous amounts of money wasted on killing machines (this term includes both people and guns). The insanity of

> *If we want peace, we must reform, restructure and strengthen the United Nations.*
>
> Dr. John Logue, 1985
> Director, Common Heritage Institute

nuclear killing machines is making us realize that World War III (with possibly 5 *billion* fatalities) may bring about the end of all people on this planet. It is the plea of *PlanetHood* that we end the arms race—not the human race.

THE FIRST FOUR STEPS

Let's briefly review the steps we've covered so far. Step One requires us to assert our ultimate human right to live in a world free from the threat of death by nuclear war. Step Two asks us to understand the new top layer of government we need in order to nail down this ultimate human right for you and your family for all time. We need to complete the governmental structure of the world with *a lawmaking body* (representing the people of the world), *a world court* (staffed with the wisest judges chosen from among the nations of the world), and *an effective system to enforce* the agreed standards of national behavior. This final layer of government would globally insure our human rights, protect the sovereignty of nation-states in internal matters, and maintain the peace.

By taking Step Three we realize what it means to become a Peace Patriot. We are urged to step into George Washington's footsteps in creating and supporting a new constitution to govern the nations of the world. The Federal Republic of the World must be strong enough to avoid ineffectiveness and weak enough to avoid tyranny. This is secured by a *wise balance of power* between the legislative, executive, and judicial branches.

In Step Four we acknowledge our enormous progress over the past century in creating international law. We note how the nations of the world are getting accustomed to working with each other—*gradually and safely* yielding small portions of their sovereignty in order to benefit from binding international agreements for the common good. We see that nation-states are already merging into larger economic and political entities to meet their common needs. *There is a growing awareness that the world system must change to meet the challenge of the 21st Century.*

> *When we get to the point, as one day we will, that both sides know that in any outbreak of general hostilities, regardless of the element of surprise, destruction will be both reciprocal and complete, possibly we will have sense enough to meet at the conference table with the understanding that the era of armaments has ended and the human race must conform its actions to this truth or die.*
>
> Dwight D. Eisenhower
> Former U.S. President
> Personal letter, April 4, 1965

In Step Five we will discuss updating our vehicle for survival—the U.N.—as we move toward an effective world system with checks and balances to protect our rights and freedoms. This step is primarily concerned with spelling out how we need to reform the U.N. to assure world peace. It does not try to describe the enormous contributions to world peace this pioneering organization has given us—even with its hands tied behind its back. Appendix 2 gives you an inspiring summary of many of its ground-breaking services to the world in the past forty years.

After the carnage of World War II with 35 million dead, many nations were determined not to go through that again. Toward the end of the war we began to plan the United Nations Organization.

In October 1945 the Charter was ratified by 50 nations at San Francisco. Enthusiasm ran high. "The U.N. Charter can be a greater Magna Carta," said John Foster Dulles, our Secretary of State who was a delegate to the San Francisco conference. It's interesting to note that the U.N. Charter was completed on June 26, 1945—six weeks before Hiroshima and Nagasaki. This may help explain its weakness.

THE SECURITY COUNCIL

The Charter provides for a Security Council and a General Assembly. The Security Council was supposed to be the enforcement arm. It has five permanent members who were victorious in World War II: the United States, the Soviet Union, Britain, France, and China (in 1971 the People's Republic of China re-

> *When there is a problem between two small nations, the problem disappears. When there is a problem between a big country and a small country, the little country disappears. When there is a problem between two big countries, the United Nations disappears.*
>
> Victor Belaunde
> Peruvian Ambassador to U.N.

placed Nationalist China on the Security Council). In addition there are now ten rotating members—originally there were six. It was deliberately set up so that the big powers could ignore any vote they didn't like. *Any one of the five permanent members of the Security Council can veto any enforcement action—even if the rest of the world is for it!*

Because of the distrust and conflict between the Soviet Union and the United States (and because we usually vote to support our friends and the Soviets usually support their friends), deadlocks on all important issues involving war and peace have usually blocked effective action by the U.N. This lack of respect for legal, peaceful conflict resolution has set a poor example for the other 157 nations of the world. Brian Urquhart, U.N. Under Secretary-General for

> *A Security Council that can be rendered impotent by the vote of one nation obviously cannot begin to guarantee security. A General Assembly that can pass resolutions with the votes of nations representing less than 10 percent of the world's population, and some 3 percent of the gross world product, will not have, and cannot get, the respect it must have if its decisions are to be taken seriously.*
>
> Dr. John Logue, December 26, 1985
> Director, Common Heritage Institute
> *A More Effective United Nations*
> New Jersey Law Journal

Special Political Affairs lamented, "There are moments when I feel that only an invasion from outer space will reintroduce into the Security Council that unanimity and spirit which the founders of the Charter were talking about."

Thus we have a toddling Security Council that under the Charter is empowered to send armed forces anywhere on earth to stop war. And it is usually rendered impotent because of the Charter requirement for the unanimous vote of the permanent members of the Security Council to act in preserving peace. In 1945 we weren't quite ready yet to take the final step.

THE GENERAL ASSEMBLY

In addition to the Security Council, the Charter of the United Nations set up the General Assembly. It has been called a "town meeting of the world" by former Secretary-General Trygve Lie. Each nation has one vote in the General Assembly which has grown from the original 50 nations to 159 today. Thus small nations, *regardless of size*, have the same vote as large nations, *regardless of population*. For example, Grenada with about 90,000 people has an equal vote with the United States which has almost 1/4 billion people.

Since the Security Council has all the power to act, the big powers gave the other nations of the world the power to talk! It's interesting to note that when a resolution passes the General Assembly, it goes to the Security Council *as a recommendation only*. The General Assembly has no Charter power to fund or require any action to keep the peace—or to do anything but recommend!

THE NEED FOR REFORM

Vernon Nash wrote in *The World Must Be Governed*, ". . . if Hamilton or any other founding father returned to the United States today and read a current article about the performance and prospects of the United Nations, he certainly would say to himself, 'This is where I came in.' . . . then, as now, men kept trying to get order without law, to establish peace while retaining the right and power to go on doing as they pleased."

The United States, which was the principal mover in creating

> *The United Nations is an extremely important and useful institution* provided *the peoples and governments of the world realize that it is merely a transitional system toward the final goal, which is the establishment of a supranational authority vested with sufficient legislative and executive powers to keep the peace.*
>
> Albert Einstein

the World Court, gave the appearance of accepting compulsory jurisdiction over "any question of international law." But that was quite deceptive. By special reservations, the U.S. excluded certain disputes which the U.S. might *by itself* decide it wanted solely within its own domestic jurisdiction.

A nation undermines the court when it gives the appearance of accepting the court, and at the same time, denies to the tribunal the normal powers of every judicial agency. *A nation which defies the jurisdiction of the court when it becomes a defendant, shows contempt for the court.* A nation which walks away from the Court when it fears a judgment against it undercuts the process of law. When these things are done by a nation that helped establish the World Court, it diminishes respect for itself. Despite technical legal arguments that were raised to justify the U.S. position when Nicaragua in 1984 complained that we were mining its harbors and seeking to overthrow its government, American refusal to honor the Court or its judgments was seen throughout the world as a hypocritical manifestation of scorn for the tribunal which the United States praised when decisions went in its favor. *Defiance of law is an invitation to disaster. What may have been tolerable in the pre-nuclear age is intolerable now.*

In a world of law and order, aggressor nations should clearly be identified as outlaws for rejecting the rule of law. This is not to suggest that justified grievances should be ignored; sincere efforts must be made to find just solutions. *But a handful of states, or a small group of fanatics, should not be permitted to thwart humankind's progress toward a more lawful and peaceful world.*

SUPPORTING THE U.N.

In 1986 the U.S. Congress reduced its financial support of the United Nations by over half, largely because it did not like certain expenditures. Since the total U.N. budget is less than New York City's, any reduction of its annual $800 million income is crippling. In the past the Soviet Union has

> *The leader of one of the great nations whose voice can be heard and listened to should go to the Assembly of the United Nations, and advocate . . . an international police force for the enforcement . . . of peace . . . all around the world.*
>
> Harry Truman, 1953
> Former U.S. President

also failed to pay U.N. bills for the same reason. In October 1987, Mikhail Gorbachev talked of invigorating the Security Council.

To back up his words, the Soviet Union announced that it will pay all its overdue U.N. bills which come to $197 million. That left the United States in October 1987 as the outstanding delinquent who still owed over $414 million, including $61 million for peacekeeping forces which the U.S. opposed.

> *We seek to strengthen the United Nations, to help solve its financial problems, to make it a more effective instrument for peace, to develop it into a genuine world security system . . . capable of resolving disputes on the basis of law, of insuring the security of the large and the small, and of creating conditions under which arms can finally be abolished . . . . This will require a new effort to achieve world law.*
>
> John F. Kennedy
> Former U.S. President

The world spends only $800 MILLION a year on peace through the U.N., and $1 TRILLION on national military budgets—**over a thousand times more!!!** Does it come as a surprise that we are today 1,000 times more effective at waging war than at waging peace?

There are amazing parallels between our situation with the United Nations today and the dangerous situation in the United States two centuries ago. Tom Hudgens in his book *Let's Abolish War* points out that the Continental Congress under the Articles of Confederation:

1. Had no independent taxing powers.
2. Could not regulate interstate and foreign commerce.
3. Had no powers of direct enforcement of its laws.
4. Was ineffective in foreign affairs.
5. Had no chief executive.
6. Had no binding court of justice . . . .

"Do you realize," Hudgens asks, "that every one of these charges can be leveled at the United Nations today? We are living today under the Articles of Confederation except we call it the United Nations."

Instead of starting all over again, reforming the U.N. may be our best bet to rapidly insure our ultimate human right. A redrafting of the Charter and its ratification by the nations of the world is needed. It won't be easy to persuade nations to mend their ways, but it can be done. *For years, the officials of the U.N. have known what needs to be done. They're powerless unless authorized by the nations of the world.* They've been waiting for you to take the needed steps to alter the views of the entrenched diplomats which would permit them to respond effectively to international lawlessness—and thus set the stage for a new era of prosperity and peace on earth.

CONFEDERATION VS. FEDERATION

In order to take Step Five by working to make the U.N. more effective in the nuclear age, you must clearly understand the key differences between the U.N. today and the World Federation we need for tomorrow. Just as the terms "Confederation" and "Federation" were confusing to the 1787 delegates at Philadelphia, people usually don't understand their significance today. The World Federalist Association in its pamphlet *We the People* helps us clarify the crucial differences between a league or confederation, and a federation or union:*

In a league or confederation (like the U.N.), each state does as it pleases regardless of the consequences to the whole; in a *federation* or *union* (like the U.S.), each state accepts some restrictions for the security of the whole.

In a league, the central body is merely a debating society without authority to control the harmful behavior of individuals; in a *federation*, the central body makes laws for the protection of the whole and prosecutes individuals who break them.

In a league, any enforcement is attempted only against member states; in a *federation*, enforcement of laws is directed against individual lawbreakers.

*A copy may be obtained from the World Federalist Association, 417 Seventh Street, S.E., Washington, D.C. 20003. Toll free phone: 1-800-HATE WAR.

In a league, conflicts among members continue unabated, resulting in costly arms races and wars; in a *federation*, conflicts among states are worked out in a federal parliament and in federal courts.

A league has no independent sources of revenue; a *federation* has its own supplemental sources of revenue.

In a league, state loyalty overrides loyalty to the wider community; in a *federation*, loyalty to each state is balanced by loyalty to the wider community.

LOOKING FOR THE BEST WAY

Could you feel secure if a congress made up of people from all over the world enacted binding international laws? Would you be taken advantage of? Too heavily taxed? Your rights ignored? Could a dictator grab power? Can we set up a world legislature, court, and executive branch that will be more protective of the U.S. than the Pentagon? How can we actually increase our "defense" through a reformed U.N.? How do we reform the U.N. to give us *unparalleled abundance*?

As George Washington and Benjamin Franklin would testify, there is no one simple way to hammer out a

This planet is in bad political shape and is administered appallingly. An outer-space inspection team would undoubtedly give us an F (failure) or a triple D (dumb, deficient and dangerous) in planetary management. Our world is afflicted by a good dozen conflicts almost permanently. Its skies, lands and oceans are infested with atomic weapons which cost humanity 850 billion dollars a year, while so many poor people are still dying of hunger on this planet. And yet, I have seen the UN become universal and prevent many conflicts. I have seen the dangerous decolonization page turned quickly and with infinitely less bloodshed than in Europe and the Americas in preceding centuries. I have seen a flowering expansion of international cooperation in thirty-two UN specialized agencies and world programs.

Robert Muller
Former U.N. Assistant Secy.-Gen.
Chancellor, University for Peace
Author, *What War Taught Me About Peace*

new constitution. It takes an open-minded willingness to consider all points of view, to lay aside one's prejudices and psychological certainties, and to be patient enough to listen and search until effective answers are found and agreed upon. Just as success in 1787 required that various states be satisfied, in like manner we must create a reformed U.N. that meets today's needs and interests of the nations of the world.

There have been many proposals to improve the United Nations and make it more effective as the keeper of the peace. One suggestion, known as the "Binding Triad," comes from Richard Hudson, founder of the Center for War/Peace Studies. It requires two basic modifications of the U.N. Charter:

> The voting system in the General Assembly would be changed. Important decisions would still be adopted with a single vote, *but with three simultaneous majorities within that vote*. Approval of a resolution would require that the majority vote include two-thirds of the members present and voting (as at present), nations representing two-thirds of the population of those present and voting, and nations representing two-thirds of the contributions to the regular U.N. budget of those present and voting. Thus, in order for a resolution to pass it would have to be supported strongly by most of the countries of the world, most of the population of the world, and most of the political/economic/military strength of the world.

> The powers of the General Assembly would be increased under the Binding Triad so that in most cases its resolutions would be binding, not recommendations as at present. The new General Assembly, now a global legislature, will be able to use peacekeeping forces and/or economic sanctions to carry out its decisions. However, the Assembly would not be permitted "to intervene in matters which are essentially within the jurisdiction of any state." If the jurisdiction were in doubt, the issue would be referred to the World Court,

and if the court ruled that the question was essentially domestic, the Assembly could not act.*

This is only one possibility for giving the General Assembly limited legislative powers. A World Constitution for the Federation of Earth has been drafted by the World Constitution and Parliament Association headed by Philip Isely of Lakewood, Colorado. There are many ways to reform the U.N. to give the world binding international laws, a binding court of international justice, and an executive branch to enforce the law with an international military force *that replaces national armies, navies, and air forces.* A 14-point program is shown on the next page. Models of new international systems to create world order have been prepared by many scholars, among which include Professor Richard Falk of Princeton University, Professor Saul Mendlovitz of Rutgers, and Professor Louis Sohn of Harvard University. With safe checks and balances, we can set up an overall system that will enable the world to work! Political leaders lack the political will to make the required changes in the U.N. It's time for the public to speak out.

> *Many of these proposals may appear unpatriotic or even treasonous to those who identify patriotism with the worship of American military power .... If patriotism is an active concern for the freedom, welfare and survival of one's people, there is no patriotic duty more immediate than the abolition of war as a national right and institution.*
>
> Cord Meyer
> *Peace or Anarchy*

Once the world union is formed, do we want to permit an easy divorce if a nation wants to get out when it disagrees about something? The American Civil War in 1861-1865 settled whether states could leave the Federal Union if they disagreed with its policies. The victory by the Union clearly established that no state could secede from the Federal Government once it agreed to be a member. If politicians in a nation become angry

*For more information and a videotape on the Binding Triad, write the Center for War/Peace Studies, 218 E. 18th Street, New York, NY 10003. Phone: (212) 475-1077.

A 14-POINT PROGRAM
for Reforming
the United Nations

1. Improve the General Assembly decision-making process.
2. Modify the veto in the Security Council.
3. Create an International Disarmament Organization.
4. Improve the dispute settlement process.
5. Improve the U.N.'s peacekeeping capability.
6. Provide for adequate and stable U.N. revenues.
7. Increase the use of the International Court of Justice.
8. Create an International Criminal Court to try hijackers and terrorists.
9. Improve the U.N.'s human rights machinery.
10. Create stronger U.N. environmental and conservation programs.
11. Provide international authorities for areas not under national control.
12. Provide for more effective world trade and monetary sytems.
13. Establish a consolidated U.N. development program.
14. Achieve administrative reform of the U.N. system.

For more details write to Campaign for U.N. Reform, 418 Seventh Street, S.E., Washington, D.C. 20003. Phone: (202) 546-3956.

and could whip up the people to get out, it would signal the end of the world system. Once a nation agrees to the reformed U.N., it must be permanent. "By resigning from the organization," Cord Meyer warns, "a nation could free itself from international supervision, forcing a renewal of the armament race and certain war. In view of the nature of the new weapons, secession would be synonymous with aggression."

As we've pointed out, *there is no one way* to transform the United Nations into an effective world government. It is important that you give thought to this vital matter and arrive at your own conclusions on how to do it. Then discuss them with your friends and neighbors who will no doubt develop their own ideas. It is only from the clash of opinions that a living truth will emerge that will point to an effective way to complete the governmental structure of the world.

THE CHALLENGE OF OUR AGE

We are at a crucial point in history. We are on the threshold of great progress. We have reached the stage where large scale wars are no longer compatible with the future of the human race. We have gone beyond the point where such military power is protective. Instead it threatens to kill us all. This calls for action.

Even if we were not threatened by nuclear war, we would benefit enormously by

> *When young people see that there are adults who work to resolve conflicts peaceably, they may be more hopeful about there being a future for them.*
>
> Mary Finn, 1984
> Kent State University

a reformed U.N. Through a world republic our children will have greater prosperity, more personal opportunities for a good life, and better protection of their human rights and freedoms.

To stop the bloodshed in the wild west of the last century, we established sheriffs and judges whose job it was to protect people from lawbreakers. This is exactly what needs to be done today. Let's take the pistols off the hips of today's 159 bristling nations and set up a world "sheriff" system. The Peacekeeping Forces of the U.N., backed by a world system of courts providing international justice, can make us all far safer than the present worldwide anarchy.

Imagine what a difference this would make in your life and that of your loved ones. The heavy taxes that spill your "economic blood" year by year would no longer be used to feed a greedy war machine. Your children could then feel confident that they will have a future. Business could be liberated from the import and export fences that limit opportunities.

> *A federation of all humanity, together with a sufficient means of social justice to ensure health, education, and a rough equality of opportunity, would mean such a release and increase of human energy as to open a new phase in human history.*
>
> H.G. Wells
> Noted Historian

We could effectively begin to improve the quality of the air we breathe and the water we drink. Education, medical care, and quality of life would vastly improve when the world no longer spent $1.5 million each minute on increasing its killing capacity. *A small international Peacekeeping Force of several hundred thousand well-trained and equipped people could replace the millions of soldiers now under arms who constantly disrupt the peace of the planet.*

Over the past several centuries there has been a gradual awakening of the importance of international law that can override the military passions of the 159 separate nations around the globe. We have tried World Courts and have found that they work if we want them to. We have set up international organizations such as the League of Nations and the United Nations. Each has been a step forward.

All this experimenting, testing, trying, and hoping *have been important steps up the ladder of international growth* toward the completion of the governmental structure of our world. We now have the glorious challenge of creating lasting peace and prosperity by reforming the United Nations into a world republic. We need not agree here on all of the details.

What is decisive is the determination to make the organization effective.

We can no longer pretend that we don't know what needs to be done. How long will it be until a president, prime minister, or general secretary calls for a Conference to Reform the United Nations or an International Constitutional Convention—and invites all nations to send delegates? Here is an opportunity for statesmanship and fame of the highest order. Let us seize this history-making opportunity and accept the challenge to create a more peaceful world.

APPROACHING PLANETHOOD

Many nations today, and eventually all nations, will be willing to cooperate in a reformed United Nations. They will respond to the insistence of their people that we not waste their tax money blowing the world apart. These nations will want to benefit from the much safer and far less costly protection of their national rights and freedoms that only a world government can offer

> The idea of a comprehensive system of security is the first plan for a possible new organization of life in our common planetary home. In other words, it is a pass into our future where security of all is a token of the security for everyone. We hope the current session of the United Nations General Assembly will jointly develop and concretise this idea.
>
> Mikhail Gorbachev
> Soviet General Secretary
> Article in *Pravda*, September 17, 1987

them. At long last, they can get out of the arms race and enjoy a much higher standard of living, education, culture, medical care, etc.

It is now time for these nations to reform the U.N. Charter. They will become a powerful force when they *unite and act together*. Sooner or later, those nations who resist at first will join in—just as holdout states discovered *they could not afford to pass up the many benefits* of becoming a part of the United States two centuries ago.

Like Paul Revere, let's awaken our neighbors. Let's give ourselves effective international law, world courts, and enforcement in a safe system of checks and balances. Let's work continuously to bring about the day when our front lines of defense consist of brigades of international attorneys practicing before a binding world court. Then we'll have finally secured our ultimate human right to live in a peaceful world free from the threat of death by nuclear war.

We need a reliable cop on the international corner. Will you help our ungoverned world to create a world system that can work? As a Peace Patriot of the 21st Century, you'll know that you have done your part to make your life count. You will have saved yourself, your family, and all of the men, women, and children throughout our beautiful planet now and for generations to come.

IT DEPENDS ON YOU!

6th Step

Tell Your Friends and Neighbors

To rescue yourself from nuclear extinction, it is important that you tell the great news to your friends and neighbors: *a safe way has been found to get rid of nuclear and other mass killing machines.* Through reform of the United Nations with improved international law, courts, and enforcement, we can give all people on planet Earth *a level of security that we lack at the present time.*

OVERCOMING FEARS AND PREJUDICES

Before we can begin to think in planetary terms, we must diminish the tensions between the Soviet Union and the United States. Despite vast differences, we are convinced that it can be done because it is in the interest of both nations. We must overcome the fears and prejudices which now divide the citizens of these two great powers.

> *There is no issue at stake in our political relations with the Soviet Union—no hope, no fear, nothing to which we aspire, nothing we would like to avoid—which could conceivably be worth a nuclear war.*
> Professor George Kennan, 1985
> Former U.S. Ambassador to Moscow

Many Americans feel that *communism and capitalism seem irreconcilable.* Marxist-Leninist doctrines have called for the

114

overthrow of the capitalist class by a revolution and dictatorship of the proletariat. Communists have harshly suppressed dissent. Private property—the means of production—belongs to the state. Organized religion is seen as the opiate of the masses and is to be discouraged or repressed.

American history books decry the violent birth of the Soviet system in 1917, when large numbers of the Russian aristocracy, land owners, and political opponents were murdered. Stalin's perfidy in signing a pact with Hitler in 1939 is not forgotten. We recall the Red Army's refusal, after World War II, to leave the countries of eastern Europe until puppet communist regimes were installed. Soviet suppression of freedom in Czechoslovakia, Hungary, and Poland is another sore point. Russia's persistent military occupation of Afghanistan, despite worldwide condemnation, has been a continuing irritant.

> *The basic reason for the frustration of efforts to disarm is that disarmament negotiations have sought to treat the symptoms of the arms race—military forces—rather than the underlying cause of the arms race—the failure of our small planet to create an alternative problem-solving system on which nations can rely for their safety. Nations have felt the need for armed forces for centuries, and it is altogether too much to ask them to disarm in a political vacuum. If they lay down their arms, how do they provide for their security?*
>
> Richard Hudson
> Director, Center for War/Peace Studies

The expansion of Soviet influence throughout the globe and the establishment of communist or socialist governments in such countries of the western hemisphere as Cuba and Nicaragua is seen as a threat to the survival of democracy. It is felt that communist subversion and Soviet expansion must be contained if vital American interests are to be preserved. We fear "falling dominoes" and loss of the American way of life.

Restrictions on emigration, suppression of dissidents, and other human rights violations add to the list of complaints. The growth of Soviet military power increases the apprehension of the United States and its allies.

The U.S. response is aimed at restoring the military balance, resisting Soviet encroachment, supporting those who oppose

Soviet transgressions, and vigorously defending U.S. interests. To achieve these objectives, American policy seeks to enhance the political, military, and economic power of the United States and its friends, and to defeat Soviet adventurism—by overt or covert opposition—wherever it may appear.

To understand the Soviet point of view, we must recall that capitalism is seen as a social system for exploiting the working class. The Russians point to American unemployment, inflation, recessions, homelessness, racism, and poverty as indicators that the oppressive and inferior capitalist system will be "buried" by history. Old Russian leaders remember that American troops were landed in Murmansk in 1918 to help overthrow the communist revolution, and that America withheld recognition of the Soviet Union until 1933. Intervention by the U.S. in the affairs of other nations is seen as an effort to preserve an unjust status quo in order to extract benefits for the rich at the expense of the poor.

The Soviet Union points to the illegal use of overt and covert military force by the United States in Vietnam, Cuba, Grenada, the Middle East, and Latin America as proof of America's militant imperialistic designs. It condemns American support for the "contras" in their war against Nicaragua as a case of blatant aggression. U.S. refusal to abide by decisions of

> *We are all students, and our teacher is life and time. I believe that more and more people will come to realize that through RESTRUCTURING in the broad sense of the word, the integrity of the world will be enhanced. Having earned good marks from our main teacher—life—we shall enter the twenty-first century well prepared and sure that there will be further progress.*
>
> Mikhail Gorbachev
> *Perestroika: New Thinking for Our Country and the World*

the World Court (which the U.S.S.R. has never accepted) is denounced as American hypocrisy. U.S. economic and military aid to repressive and dictatorial regimes is seen as further proof of American malevolence.

The growth of American weaponry on land, sea, and in the air, the deployment of nuclear missiles all around the Soviet Union, as well as plans to build an impenetrable shield in space, are viewed by the Soviets as U.S. treaty-breaking, and preparation for a first-strike nuclear war. The memory of 20 million countrymen killed in World War II sustains their concern about American armaments.

PEACEFUL COEXISTENCE

Despite their apprehensions, Soviet leaders have spoken out for a reduction of tensions and have branded the idea of winning a nuclear war as "dangerous madness." President Reagan has reached the same conclusion. In February 1984, the Soviet Chairman, addressing the Central Committee of the Communist Party, proclaimed "the principle of peaceful coexistence of states with different social systems." He went on to declare, "We need no military superiority. We do not intend to dictate our will to others . . . . We are for a peaceful settlement of all disputable international problems through serious, equal, and constructive talks."

The differences between the U.S. and the U.S.S.R. certainly do not justify either side risking the future of humankind in order to achieve its own particular ends. The U.S. Secretary of State George Shultz said: "A peaceful world order does not require that we and the Soviet Union agree on all the fundamentals of morals or politics." Both the United States and the Soviet Union clearly recognize the need for mutual cooperation. General Secretary Gorbachev has called for "New Thinking" for the Soviet Union and the world. He has embraced many of the goals for which America has always stood. His sincerity should be tested and verified. *Differences in ideology should not blind nations to the need for all human beings to live in peace.*

> *World government is not an "ultimate goal" but an immediate necessity. In fact, it has been overdue since 1914. The convulsions of the past decades are the clear symptoms of a dead and decaying political system.*
>
> Emery Reves
> *The Anatomy of Peace*

WE CAN BE FRIENDS

Despite ideological differences, the United States enjoys good relations with many nations of different political persuasion—socialist, communist, or dictatorial. We make friendly overtures to such Soviet allies as communist Poland, Hungary, and Romania. The fact that China has a dedicated communist government does not prevent the United States from now being on good terms with that ancient land. The presence of a militant communist country, Cuba, ninety miles off the U.S. coast, does not visibly detract from the security or welfare of American citizens on the mainland. Our recent history and our alliances with Germany, Italy, and Japan have demonstrated that even former enemies in war can become friends in peace. *Russia and America were allies in war; they should be friends in peace.*

If we look beyond the bristling rhetoric (often intended for local political consumption) and see the broader objectives which both the American and Soviet leaders have clearly recognized, a workable accommodation through reasonable compromise should be possible. What is needed is for the leaders of both nations to do as George Washington and the U.S. Founding Fathers did: to muster the will, wisdom, determination, patience, and courage to take the necessary specific steps toward the declared common goals.

> *It is strange: one could not envisage for a moment a household, a city, a school, a firm, a factory, a farm, an institution, a religion, or a nation without a head, a principal, a manager, an administrator, or a government. But we accept readily that the world can be left without one! We should not be surprised, therefore, that there are so many wars, acts of violence, and global crises on this planet.*
>
> **Robert Muller**
> Former U.N. Assistant Secy.-Gen.
> Chancellor, University for Peace
> Author, *A Planet of Hope*

We must learn to overcome traditional hostilities and the habit of identifying all citizens with the policies of their government. Nothing constructive is achieved by the fruitless belaboring of past misdeeds—*which were generated by leaders who have long since passed from the scene.* Adding venom to a poisoned wound cures nothing. The vilification of whole nations is a dehumanizing distortion of reality.

If this world is to achieve planethood and not fall to disaster, both the right wing and the left wing must learn to work in harmony. What is important is not the hard line or the soft line, but the line that leads to peace.

ELIMINATE THE ARMS RACE

You can help people understand that we must rapidly reform the United Nations with a world legislature, a world court system, and an executive branch capable of enforcing the law and maintaining the peace. Today's fifty thousand nuclear devices do not give us security—they are the greatest danger humanity has known. An improved world system *will make it safe* to eliminate the arms race which costs about $1.5 million per minute worldwide.

> *Henceforth, every nation's foreign policy must be judged at every point by one consideration: does it lead us to a world of law and order or does it lead us back to anarchy and death?*
>
> Albert Einstein

We should all make sure that our tax dollars are used for the benefit—and not for the death—of society. For every billion dollars spent on death devices, we create about 28,000 jobs. That same amount of money could create 71,000 jobs if spent for education, and 57,000 jobs if used to buy goods and services. Surely, it is in everyone's interest to spend money for living rather than dying. Few people understand the great abundance we can create when we get rid of our dependence on costly killing machines. There is incredible waste (as well as corruption) in the production of redundant military systems for overlapping military services. According to Rear Admiral Gene R. LaRocque, U.S. Navy (Ret.), "Weapons are often purchased primarily for the benefit of major military contractors, not for the defense of the United States. In the absence of effective competition in the military industry, the profit motive gives companies the incentive to sell as many weapons at as high a price as possible." Furthermore, much of the world's scientific brain power is being squandered on weapons of mass destruction, instead of being used for vital human betterment.

STAR WARS WILL NOT SAVE US

Your fellow citizens must understand that it is more sensible and much cheaper to *eliminate nuclear missiles* than to squander countless hundreds of billions trying to build a shield in outer space which—some hope—may intercept some of the incoming nuclear missiles before they destroy the target and its inhabitants. The outrageously expensive Star Wars, even if it works, *will not stop low flying nuclear projectiles that can be launched from submarines, surface ships, planes, or from neighboring countries—and still wipe out every American city.*

A Tomahawk cruise missile launched from a submarine can travel up to 1500 miles. It travels inside the atmosphere—sneaking under the Star Wars detecting sensors. When the people who are running the Star Wars program are asked specific questions, they state that it will not shield our country as some claim. They only expect it to be effective to "protect" certain areas such as a few military installations. Even such protection is not 100%.

> *There is deception and mismanagement at the highest levels in the Department of Defense.*
> Senator Lowell Weicker, Jr.
> March 27, 1987
> Ranking Republican
> Senate Appropriations Committee

As in other nuclear matters our citizens are not being told the complete truth. It is estimated to cost over a trillion dollars, and like many military estimates, it will probably run much more—to say nothing of the cost of staffing and maintaining it. And what about the clouds of nuclear death that will engulf the planet should nuclear missiles be exploded in outer space? The nuclear shroud will fall on all of us. Star Wars can bankrupt us—but it cannot save us from nuclear extinction.

Both Dr. Helen Caldicott and President Dwight Eisenhower put the blame for our nuclear madness on what political scientists call the Iron Triangle—the military, the politicians, and the industrialists that profit in the millions. The responsibility should *also rest with each of us who neglects to do what we can to correct the situation.*

The military is doing what it's trained to do. Whether in the Kremlin or the Pentagon, commanders must assume that "the enemy" intends to attack. Naturally, they want more and better weapons all the time. A good way to get more is to publicly underestimate their own strength while exaggerating that of their adversary.

Human beings forget to be human. It is up to YOU to make it clear to people around you that war is not a glorious game and a "casualty" is not merely a statistic. It is YOUR son, YOUR daughter, YOUR husband, YOUR wife, YOUR friend, and YOU! When the military asks for billions of dollars of your money for a weapon of mass destruction, demand to know how many *people* it will kill and *who* those people are likely to be, and *why* they deserve such a fate. Insist upon an answer. If you don't care enough to act, you must share the blame.

> *All of us here would like very much to defend the people of the United States. And the President has come up with a vision. If you could meet his vision, which says you will make nuclear weapons impotent—get rid of all nuclear weapons—and will defend the United States, we'd all buy this if it could be done. But the problem with the President's vision is none of this stuff they're trying to do works. The whole SDI is really very seductive, but it is as fraudulent as it is seductive.*
>
> Rear Admiral Gene R. La Rocque
> U.S. Navy (Ret.)
> The Center for Defense Information
> December 13, 1987

The U.S. military purse is controlled by the Congress, and Congress is controlled by the people. It is up to *you*, the informed voters, *to stop robbing the hungry and the poor to feed an insatiable war machine.* Between 1960 and 1980, worldwide military expenditures nearly doubled. The expenditure curve for arms is ever upward. World military budgets now exceed TWO BILLION DOLLARS EACH DAY! What is so ironic and tragic is that these enormous

> *Don't trust government statements. They fit the facts to fit the policy*
> William J. Fulbright
> Former Chairman, U.S. Senate
> Foreign Relations Committee
> On his 80th birthday

military expenditures do not enhance national security—they undermine it. There can be no winner of a nuclear war; everybody loses and loses everything.

THE STRENGTH OF A NATION

The strength of a nation does not solely depend upon its capacity to destroy other nations and kill their citizens. True national security is dependent upon the spirit of its people, their respect for the integrity of their leaders, and their confidence in the justness of their government. When people are lied to or taken advantage of, the government will lack their respect and lose power—despite the vastness of its military arsenal. As long as significant portions of the population feel that they are mere pawns in a dangerous costly game of the politicians, the military, and the industrialists, the vital stamina, unity, and determination of the nation will be destroyed.

Imagine what would happen if the U.S. and the Soviets were blessed at the same time with leaders who were determined and able to implement their declared goal of complete disarmament under effective international controls. *Imagine the savings being used to retrain displaced workers, stimulate new industries, get rid of national debt and deficits, lower taxes, and improve housing, education, and medical care for the citizens of both superpowers—and to help raise the standard of living in underdeveloped countries.*

Such action would be hailed with wild enthusiasm among people all over the world! There would be an unprecedented outburst of affection and appreciation to both nations for having begun to live up to their professed desire to serve the interests of humankind. Would the national security of either the U.S. or the Soviet Union be diminished? Quite the contrary! Economic stability and growth enhances national security. Would the popularity of the national leaders among their own people be reduced? Surely not! Opinion polls following the summit meeting in Washington in December 1987 showed that the popularity of both Reagan and Gorbachev soared when they reached an arms agreement.

The great reduction of military expenses (made possible by a reformed U.N. capable of maintaining peace in the world) would eliminate the U.S. budget deficit. We could then begin to pay off our enormous national debt. And it could enable us to gradually reverse our big trade deficit by producing better civilian products instead of better ways to kill off humanity. It would enable the Soviets to produce more consumer goods and thereby serve their own people better. Japan, *whose Constitution prohibits massive armaments*, has risen from the ashes of defeat in World War II to demonstrate that today economic power is more important than military power.

> *The exercise by some nation-states of their as-yet-unlimited right to lie, assassinate, terrorize and wage war, and to justify these actions in the name of "national security," causes many to despair for the future of our planet. But there is a solution to this problem of international anarchy: A common security system for all nations under enforceable world law.*
>
> Myron W. Kronisch
> Campaign for U.N. Reform

Since the consequences of disarmament are so obviously desirable from every point of view, it is an insult to human intelligence to believe that such reasonable goals are unattainable. If we are to dwell together in peace on this interdependent planet, traditional perceptions of self-interest based on military power must be relegated to a bygone age. *All of humankind must be brought under the protective shield of an enlightened planethood.*

SOLVING INTERNATIONAL PROBLEMS

It is important that your friends and neighbors understand that the preservation of our planet for human habitation requires that we add a final layer of international government to get rid of the international anarchy we have today. *International problems must have international solutions.*

> *There is one overriding truth in this nuclear age—no nation can achieve security by itself.... Security in the nuclear age means common security. This has been the central conclusion of our commission.*
>
> Cyrus Vance, 1982
> Former U.S. Secretary of State
> *Common Security A Blueprint for Survival*

Here is a partial list of the challenges we face that *can be solved only by an international government:*

- Millions killed by ongoing wars.
- Intolerable military budgets that deprive the citizens of the world.
- International terrorism.
- Acid rain from one country that destroys forests in neighboring nations.
- Nuclear pollution of the air. (It is known today that everyone on earth now has tiny amounts of radioactive nuclear particles in his or her body from the debris of bomb tests, the escape of radioactive materials into the air, etc.)
- The destruction of the oceans and marine life.
- Contagious and infectious diseases that spread across national borders.
- Ravaging the planet's minerals, oil supply, and other natural resources.
- Tariffs that impede the flow of goods and services internationally.
- The depletion of the ozone layer which sustains life on earth.

This interdependent world cannot function effectively without international cooperation and a willingness to give and take.

A world republic can increase educational, cultural, and business opportunities for people throughout the globe. It can sponsor the cooperative exploration of the frontiers of space. *It can enable our human dreams to come true.*

A NEW ERA OF HUMAN HAPPINESS

We can help our friends understand that planethood *for the first time* will enable all people to enjoy the abundance that modern technology can provide—instead of the curse of nuclear weapons that threatens to eliminate us. It can open up a new era in the unfolding of the creative, artistic, and spiritual potentials that lie within all of us. It can enormously increase our level of happiness and well-being upon this earth.

> *The popes of the nuclear age, from Pius XII through John Paul II, have affirmed pursuit of international order as the way to banish the scourge of war from human affairs.*
>
> Pastoral Letter of
> U.S. Catholic Bishops, 1983

It is important for all of us to realize that the true patriots of today must look at the world with an international breadth of mind. The "life, liberty, and pursuit of happiness" set forth in the Declaration of Independence in 1776 can only be attained in the 21st Century through the completion of a new world structure. These rights do not belong only to Americans. *They belong to everyone on this planet.*

The Peace Patriots of the 21st Century will be those who realize that human survival is a race between planethood and nuclear catastrophe. Since you now possess this knowledge and understanding, it is your responsibility to pass on a new global view of humankind. We must help those whose thoughts are still stuck in the "wild west" ruts of settling problems by mass killing.

International anarchy, NO.
Law and order, YES!

7th
Step

Do Your
Daily
Deed
for Peace

We have seen that after the horrors of each world war, nations recognized—at least for a brief time—that change was necessary to create a peaceful world order. World War I produced the Covenant of the League of Nations; World War II gave us the U.N. Charter. Both contained high ideals and the implied promise that war would be outlawed. It was not that those in authority did not know what was required; that had been carefully set forth for years by competent, dedicated political experts. *The truth is that our political leaders simply did not dare enough—or care enough. We, the public, did not do enough. We all let each other down.*

> *We need first and foremost a world democracy, a government of this planet for the people and by the people. But the problem is so colossal and unprecedented that few political thinkers even dare to consider it. They feel more at ease discussing the number and strength of missiles needed to protect specific national corrals. Since government and institutions are so slow and reluctant to do it, we must build the world community through individual commitment and action.*
>
> Robert Muller
> Former U.N. Assistant Secy.-Gen.
> Chancellor, University for Peace
> Author, *A Planet of Hope*

In today's fast moving world, important decision-makers have little time to think. Since government leaders are thus far unable to meet the challenge of creating a peaceful world, it is up to you and other peace-loving people to take action to achieve the necessary reforms. *Remember, if the people lead, the leaders will follow.*

YOUR DAILY DEED

Since we don't know how much time we have before today's unstable situation explodes on us, we must move rapidly. Our lives are at risk due to a possible computer malfunction giving a false alarm, or a political or military fanatic who triggers a chain of events that destroys humanity. Let us resolve to create a chain of events that can save humanity.

To start a chain to rescue yourself from nuclear extinction and achieve the benefits of planethood, we suggest that you pledge to yourself and the world to do a daily deed: a daily action that will make world peace one step closer when the *law of force* is replaced by the *force of law.*

Such a Peace Patriot pledge need not be burdensome. Depending upon your time and money available, you can live out your pledge *with integrity each day* on either a maximum or a minimum basis—or something in between. For example, as a daily deed you could write a letter to a friend about U.N. reform. Or you could phone a friend and discuss what you can do to help bring about U.N. reform and other needed changes. You might donate $1.00 or more to one of the organizations working for U.N. reform listed in Appendix 1 or to any other organization working for planethood.

> *Better active today than radioactive tomorrow.*

Remember the amount is not as important as *doing something every day.* You might choose to hand out this book to at least one person per day. With your neighbors you could divide a shipment of 1000 copies which can be purchased at the nonprofit price of 50¢ each postpaid. (See Page 4.) Then all you'd have to do is hand out one book each day or leave one in a public place such as a doctor's office, an airport lounge, or someone's doorstep. You could offer this book to a passerby on the street, mail it to a friend or relative, or send a copy to decision-makers or influential people in the news (libraries can usually furnish you with addresses from reference books).

You may choose to photocopy the Proclamation Form provided in Appendix 4. Then for your daily deed for peace you could gather signatures from people who wish to assert their Ultimate Human Right, and mail them to the U.N. If done day by day, this could have a great synergistic impact!

Your daily contribution can be done in a way that gives you a satisfying feeling that your life is really helping to give humanity a future. If your funds are minimal at this time, *each day* you can put at least one cent into a box labeled "Planethood." If this is all you could contribute daily, over a

> *If we fail to seize the moment, history will never forgive us—if there is a history.*
> Thomas A. Watson, 1987
> Former U.S. Ambassador to Moscow

period of a year it would total $3.65. Even this amount would help a group to promote a world system of governance. If you are fortunate enough to have more money and view this donation as *an investment in your future*, you might dedicate a percentage of your dollars to helping the cause of permanent peace and plenty. After all, of what use is your money if the world gets blown up in the next few years?*

The important thing is to resolve to do your daily deed for peace. And since the need is urgent, we suggest that your

---

*For each tax-deductible donation of $3.00 that you contribute to The Vision Foundation (Planethood Program), a free copy of *PlanetHood* will be mailed or delivered to people throughout the U.S. and the world using carefully selected mailing lists. If you have a mailing list you want used for books covered by your donation, send it in zip code order on gummed Avery labels with $3 per book. You may wish to organize fund-raising activities to get donations for this important activity. They should be sent to The Vision Foundation (Planethood Program), 700 Commercial Avenue, Coos Bay, OR 97420.

commitment to yourself and the world be for seven days a week—52 weeks in the year until world governance is achieved. Your helping the world has great consequences, and you can do it as an enjoyable project that deeply builds your self-esteem and feeling of patriotism. You can avoid treating those who disagree with you as an enemy. You can learn to increasingly keep your heart and mind open. You can disagree without being disagreeable—and at the same time do what you know is necessary to save humanity.

Rearrange the priorities in your life so that you are a real power for peace. As a modern Peace Patriot, pick the activities for which you have the most energy. And although the situation is urgent, we can maintain a reasonable balance so that we do not neglect our jobs or families in ways that undermine the wholeness of our lives. If all of us follow through on the commitment of one deed for peace each day, the job will get done. As Aesop's fable showed, the race was not won by the rabbit who traveled in great spurts; it was won by the tortoise who kept going and going and going . . . .

WAGE PEACE—NOT WAR

Planethood means learning to think in terms of a new world system of governance rather than "defense" or military systems. We must all strive to create a "peace consciousness" on the global level. Perhaps you will want to organize a local U.N. reform group or join an existing organization working for peace. You could contact one of the organizations listed in Appendix 1 and find out how you can support its activities.

> *Blessed are the peacemakers: for they shall be called the children of God.*
> Christ in the Sermon on the Mount

You could play a part in helping the people of this earth become acquainted with each other. Traveling in foreign lands as a planethood ambassador for friendship and peace can be an interesting way to follow through on your daily commitment.

Cultural and educational exchanges, and sharing scientific, business, and vocational skills can help correct false images that may have been created by their politicians or ours in the past.

Whenever you notice folks from another country visiting your city, you might ask if they're aware of the work now being done to support a new approach to lasting world peace. Almost everyone appreciates friendly, caring energy when they are in a foreign land. They might also furnish you with names of people in their nation you can write to as your daily deed for peace.

Many exchanges are taking place. For example, there are regular private meetings in Moscow between American and Soviet lawyers. American and Soviet doctors researching the medical problems of nuclear fallout have shared a Nobel Peace Prize. Soviet and American astronauts have in the past gone into space together. Private American citizens have joined Soviet scientists to set up seismic tests to measure nuclear blasts. Americans are now cruising down the Volga River, while Russians are boating down the Mississippi. There is a "Kids-to-Kids" exchange. The Association for Humanistic Psychology organized a people-to-people exchange of letters and snapshots with folks in the Soviet Union. Such friendly and constructive contacts can lead to improved human-to-human feelings and understanding.

EDUCATE FOR PEACE

As part of your daily deeds for peace, you might check on what your local elementary schools, high schools, and colleges are doing to educate for peace. Literature classes can read about war and peace, philosophy classes can examine the ethics of nuclear deterrence, and psychology and social science classes can examine the hu-

> *To reach peace, teach peace.*
> Pope John Paul II

man and social costs of warfare. History classes can study what has and hasn't worked in the past to keep peace among nations.

132

Music classes can learn to sing anthems not only for nations, but for all humankind. The problems of war and peace touch every field of study. The senior author has has just established an interdisciplinary Peace Center at Pace University Law School where he teaches The International Law of Peace.*

> A change in public opinion is always the first condition for a change in institutions. Our tragedy is that the power of the press, radio and television is used exclusively to propagate disarmament, alliances, deterrents, containments, nonaggression pacts and other treaty arrangements which, in our time and age, are thoroughly irrelevant and outdated. There can be no doubt that, if it were possible to clarify the fundamental principles of peace through the mass media, to discuss its meaning and how to obtain it, an overwhelming majority of mankind would enthusiastically endorse policies and measures integrating the sovereign nation-states into a higher legal order.
>
> Emery Reves
> The Anatomy of Peace

"A total of 235 U.S. institutions of higher learning," according to the World Policy Institute, "were offering majors, minors or concentrations in peace studies during the 1986-87 academic year; and 46 percent of all U.S. colleges and universities taught at least one course in the field, up from 14.6 percent in 1979. There are also currently at least 25 graduate programs in peace and conflict studies."**

*For a brochure describing its activities write to the Pace Peace Center, Pace University School of Law, 78 North Broadway, White Plains, NY 10603.

**Many excellent learning and teaching tools are available through Professors Burns H. Weston at the University of Iowa, Iowa City, IA 52242; Richard A. Falk and Johan Galtung of Princeton University, NJ 08540; Saul Mendlovitz of Rutgers University, New Brunswick, NJ 08903; Kenneth and Elise Boulding of the University of Colorado, Boulder, CO 80302; Dietrich Fischer of New York University, New York, NY 10003; Carolyn Stephenson of University of Hawaii at Manoa, Honolulu, HI 96822; Betty Reardon, Teachers College, Columbia University, NY 10027; John Whitely of the University of California at Irvine, Irvine, CA 92664; and World Policy Institute, 777 U.N. Plaza, New York, NY 10017. All of these scholars are teaching the advantages of an alternative security system based on ridding ourselves of world anarchy and settling disputes without war.

Students on all levels must be helped to develop factual, informed, and ethical perceptions regarding international problems. They must understand the responsibilities of being citizens in a world experiencing massive technological, economic, and political transitions. *They must learn that there are life-expanding alternatives to the present system of armed violence and killing.* Our young people are the seeds, the promises that can grow into the peaceful leaders of tomorrow.

MAKE IT HAPPEN

The moral and ethical teachings of religious groups of all faiths must become a part of our reeducational process for peace. ("Thou shalt not kill." "Love one another.") Our personal ideas of serving Jesus, God, or Allah must not mislead us into blowing up the planet and killing everyone. Instead, in the name of that which is holy to each of us, let's forgive, open our hearts, and create peace on earth with goodwill toward all.

> *Resolve that to insure world peace and disarmament among nations, we United Methodists of the Rocky Mountain Conference urge the President and the Congress of the United States, in concert with all other willing nations, to call a World Constitutional Convention to reform the United Nations into a federal, representative world government . . . .*
>
> United Methodist Church, 1983
> Rocky Mountain Conference

A 1983 pastoral letter of U.S. Catholic Bishops, and a similar letter issued by Methodist Bishops in 1986, called for a reformed international structure to meet the needs of the nuclear age. The popes of the nuclear age, from Pius XII through John Paul II, have affirmed pursuit of international order as the way to banish the devastation of war from human affairs.

There must be an end to the glorification of killing and violence. The young should not be taught to kill for old slogans. ("My country right or wrong, but right or wrong, my country.") Children must learn that it is far nobler to live for humankind than to die for the glory of a particular ruler, nation, or sect. Visiting

Heads of State could be greeted not by the traditional twenty-one gun military salute, but by songs and flowers.

All the modern means of molding public opinion—the schools, religious institutions, TV, radio, newspapers, and magazines—as well as private organizations and individuals—must get on the new bandwagon to accelerate our world along the path of peace. We can have great influence when we are carried forward by a determination to achieve permanent peace—through law and order.

The creative minds of people everywhere can rapidly begin to develop a passion for peace. Within less than a year we can create a grassroots groundswell to reorganize our international relations so that we may all live in peace and dignity. The genius of the human intellect and the caring in our hearts will find the most suitable solutions. Through your pledge to yourself that you'll not go to sleep any night until you have completed your daily deed for peace, you can help it all happen.

TRADE AND AID

No nation wishes to antagonize or go to war with an important trading partner on whom its own welfare depends. Japan and the Federal Republic of Germany were enemies of the United States not too long ago. Today we are all customers of each others' goods, and the ties of friendship and alliance are strong.

Expansion of international business can create friendships and cooperation that help to improve our human relationships with other people on this planet. The American industrialist Armand Hammer, who brought medical supplies to Russia after the revolution, continues to do business there as a valued old friend.

> *I think trade is going to be one of the main means of solving problems between the United States and the Soviet Union.*
> Donald Kendall
> Chairman of Pepsico
> Co-chairman of the American-Soviet Trade and Economic Council

Aid to countries in need can add to international goodwill. Whether it be disaster relief, or financial aid to developing countries, *both the recipient and the donor can acquire a sense of kinship* in the knowledge that they are participating in the enhancement of human caring and dignity. Let's stop using aid primarily for increasing killing power and creating military alliances. Let the human heart be our guide.

SPEAK AND ACT FOR PEACE

Never underestimate the power of the determined individual! The inspiring example of Mahatma Gandhi's courageous and successful stand against the British empire is well-known. Civil rights and women's rights have been achieved because people had the courage to speak out. Young people in the United States proved that they could change the course of a war by peaceful protests against the inhumanity of the Vietnam war. "Hell, No! We Won't Go!" became a rallying cry that helped end a war.

Each concerned citizen has a role to play. What that role may be will depend upon individual interests and skills. Some may only be able to express an opinion in private. Others may write a letter, sign a petition, or write a book. You may choose to join or lead a march, make a speech, or teach a class. You may donate your time to a worthy group that seeks a peaceful world.

> *The United Nations will have to be reformed or it will collapse into total irrelevance and nuclear war will follow.*
> Carlos P. Romulo, 1984
> Phillipine Statesman

Some have pledged their fortunes, or a portion of their incomes, to the cause of peace.

Prominent California attorney Franklin Stark and his vibrant wife Carlyn have toured America in a van while preaching peace along the way. Captain Tom Hudgens flies across the country distributing his exciting book, *Let's Abolish War: We Need L.A.W.*, that passionately pleads for world government.

Many celebrities campaign for peace. Famous pediatrician and octogenarian Dr. Benjamin Spock gets arrested for peace by climbing fences of missile sites which threaten genocide; Barbra Streisand sings for peace; actor Paul Newman speaks for peace; Yehudi Menuhin plays his violin for peace. Gregory Peck starred in a movie about peace called *Amazing Grace and Chuck*. Daniel Ellsberg, former Pentagon official, today works for peace. Garry Davis, son of a famous band leader, earned worldwide notoriety when he declared himself a "world citizen" and issued thousands of "World Government" passports.

Some run for peace; some march for peace. Mayor Larry Agran of Irvine, California, heads a coalition of a thousand local officials organized to demand that funds be allocated to cities rather than wasted on armaments. He and Michael Shuman head the Center for Innovative Diplomacy, 17931 Sky Park Circle, Irvine, CA 92714. They publish a Bulletin of Municipal Foreign Policy that notes the impact of foreign policy decisions on local communities.

> *Our goals are those of the U.N.'s founders, who sought to replace a world at war with one where the rule of law would prevail, where human rights were honored, where development would blossom, where conflict would give way to freedom from violence.*
>
> U.S. President Ronald Reagan
> Address to the U.N. General Assembly
> September 26, 1983

NETWORK FOR PEACE

Throughout the world, thousands of organizations, institutions, and private groups of various sizes and strengths are dealing with problems of peace. *They are springing up like antibodies created by nature to cure a sick organism. They need all the help they can get if the patient is to survive.**

*See *Peace Catalogue—A Guidebook to a Positive Future*. Seattle: Press for Peace, 1984.

The Consortium on Peace Research, Education and Development (COPRED), George Mason University, Fairfax, VA 22030, provides linkage and information to hundreds of members throughout America. Global Education Associates, 475 Riverside Drive, New York, NY 10115, led by Pat and Gerald Mische, authors of the inspiring book, *Toward a Human World Order*, contribute hope and information in a broad area. Many women's and church groups actively pursue goals of peace.

A growing number of institutions in Europe, India, and Asia are dedicated to peace research and promotion. Foundations and individuals support peace activities throughout the world. A United Nations University began operating in Tokyo in 1975. A University for Peace was established in Costa Rica in 1983. Its unpaid Chancellor is our friend Robert Muller, whose inspiring words are quoted throughout this book. A Peace Institute in honor of President Harry Truman exists at the Hebrew University in Jerusalem.

> *Recent history suggests that military powers—regardless of ideology—will take constructive steps toward global security only if an energetic public, in many parts of the world, insists that together we subordinate the pursuit of national power and wealth to the call for human survival and dignity.*
>
> Robert C. Johansen, 1984
> World Policy Institute

In 1985, the U.S. Congress established the United States Institute of Peace which has just begun to grant public funds for research on peace and conflict resolution. The Canadian government now sponsors a very promising Institute for Peace and Security. Computer technology is just beginning to pull the peace net together.

These loose strands that now float on a vast sea must be strengthened, drawn together, and woven into more effective networks if we are to catch the prize of peace.

Your personal commitment to the daily deed for peace can make the difference between our planet surviving or not surviving. How you think about world peace and your own daily

138

deeds will be noticed—and will inspire other people. Just as hate is transmitted from person to person like a virus, feelings of planethood—understanding, heart-to-heart cooperation, and caring—are also very contagious. From your life activities, your energy can inspire others, and thereby multiply a thousandfold as you fulfill your daily commitment to yourself and to the world.

> The world no longer has a choice between force and law. If civilization is to survive, it must choose the rule of law.
> Dwight D. Eisenhower
> Former U.S. President

Think globally—act locally. It's up to you! You can empower yourself to save the world!

8th Step

**Give
Yourself
a
Peace
Prize!**

The eight steps we've formulated to avoid nuclear extinction will take time and patience. But do we have any other way? As each of us realizes that our energy and personal power is essential to bring about permanent world peace through world law, we can feel that our lives are beginning to count in the most dangerous crisis that has ever faced humankind. We're beginning to understand:

If it is to be,
it's up to me!

It is within your power to save the world for yourself, your family, your friends, and all the people yet to live. You'll deserve a Peace Prize if you help to replace our perilous international anarchy with a secure system of international governance.

GOALS OF GOVERNMENT

We have seen that humankind is not simply moving in a vicious killing circle; it is on *an upward climb* toward completing the governmental structure of the world. We are inspired by our great progress toward planethood.

What do we want from our governments (whether city, county, state, national, or international)? *We want them to shield*

142

us from harm, protect our rights and freedoms, and make it possible to live in a degree of comfort and dignity. A government must neither be too weak nor too strong. It must be designed to be fair and impartial so that both minorities and majorities realize that they are better off to rely on laws and courts than to use violence—even though they don't always get what they want when they want it.

The Founding Fathers of the United States in 1787 invented a new form of federal government that *combines* existing state governments with an overall federal governing power. Since the U.S. federal government can enforce its laws by direct action against individual citizens, *it does not have to depend on states or declare war on a state in order to enforce a policy for the common benefit of all.* It can simply punish individual wrongdoers that have violated a federal law. We use this ingenious political structure that has worked for two hundred years to govern as many as fifty states from Florida to Alaska to Hawaii.

> *World Federalists hold before us the vision of a unified mankind living in peace under a just world order . . . The heart of their program—a world under law—is realistic and attainable.*
>
> U Thant
> Former U.N. Secretary-General

The U.S. federal government in coordination with city, county, and state governments *all harmonize together* to protect our rights as citizens to enjoy the highest level of freedom consistent with the freedom of others. We can similarly design our international government so that it is equally protective of our freedom *as individuals and as nations.*

A World Government and World Court can protect each nation's right to decide matters that affect its own people within its own borders. Through planethood each of the 159 nations on earth can enjoy the safety of being a member of a larger international community with laws, courts, and enforcement *that can give them more security than they now have*—and much more prosperity and other good things in life.

We are smart enough to create an improved international system with checks and balances and a division of power that can make nations safer than they are today from takeover by a dictator. We can build our future by learning from the mistakes and successes of the past. As day follows night, we have the power to move from the present darkness into the sunlight.

TOWARD A GOVERNED WORLD

The world is changing because the present system doesn't work. Unbridled sovereignty is being gradually restricted by the need for coping with common problems on a global basis. We're becoming aware of the sacred whole of our wonderful world.

> *World Government is not only possible, it is inevitable; and when it comes, it will appeal to patriotism in its truest, in its only sense, the patriotism of men who love their national heritages so deeply that they wish to preserve them in safety for the common good.*
>
> Peter Ustinov
> Renowned Actor

Binding rules already govern much of the environment and outer space. New international tribunals settle a host of problems by peaceful means. The processes of mediation and conciliation are being improved. Both inside and outside the United Nations, the need for U.N. reform has been recognized and is being slowly implemented. It is up to you to increase the grassroots people-to-people support of U.N. reform so that it may remove the "need" for the wasteful "defense" expenditures that are costing a million and a half dollars per minute. *Unless we destroy all weapons of mass destruction, the weapons will destroy us all.*

In "Reality and Guarantees for a Secure World" published in *Pravda* on September 17, 1987, Mikhail Gorbachev wrote:

> I do not venture to foretell how the system of all embracing security would appear in its final form. It is only clear that it could become a reality only if all means of mass annihilation were destroyed. We propose that all this be pondered by an independent commission of

144

experts and specialists, which would submit its conclusions to the United Nations Organization . . . .

We are arriving at the conclusion that wider use should be made of the institution of United Nations military observers and United Nations peace-keeping forces in disengaging the troops of warring sides, observing ceasefire and armistice agreements.

We stand on the brink of great new solutions. The Soviet Union, the United States, and other countries are beginning to realize that something must be done—urgently and quickly. We must replace fear with action that builds confidence. As former U.S. President Franklin D. Roosevelt said in another context, "We have nothing to fear but fear itself."

> There is no salvation for civilization, or even the human race, other than the creation of a world government.
>
> Albert Einstein

Although the lights of progress may sometimes flicker, the trend toward an integrated, coordinated, and more humane world is clearly discernible to the penetrating eye. Noting the unprecedented strides toward world law made during this century, we should recall that *each one was a step taken for the first time since humans began to walk the face of the earth.*

Exaggerated emphasis on the frailties of the present U.N. and World Court encourages unjustified cynicism and skepticism. It erodes the public confidence needed to stimulate the improvements that are required. We must take heart from our accomplishments—and never lose faith because of temporary defeats. There is much to be done. *Complacency and leaving the job to others can snatch defeat from victory.*

WINDING DOWN THE ARMS RACE

We cannot stop an arms race without halting the production of arms. Since our capacity to destroy human life exceeds the number of human beings available to be killed, it makes no sense to continue to expand the superfluous destructive capacity. The history of the world shows that when politicians and the military spend large amounts on armaments, their minds will somehow sooner or later find an excuse to use the killing machines for "defense." We must go beyond the ancient theory that the only way to achieve peace is to hold a big gun to someone's head!

If nuclear weapons are not usable because they will destroy all civilization, it is fair to ask: "Of what use are such unusable weapons?" The theory of deterrence is based on the logic that if nations remain vulnerable, they are safe because neither side can afford to attack first—mutual assured destruction. But countless wars show how the military becomes overconfident (the attack on Pearl Harbor was an example of overconfidence). Our security cannot be allowed to depend upon a policy that is ecocidal (destroying the environment) as well as suicidal. Those who support the argument that armaments are essential for deterrence often cite the Latin maxim: "If you want peace, prepare for war." But ancient Rome did not anticipate the nuclear age. History shows that those who prepared for war usually got what they prepared for.

IF YOU WANT PEACE, PREPARE FOR PEACE!

EXERCISE YOUR POLITICAL MUSCLE

Most important: Use your political power! What every person in a democratic society can and must do is: VOTE, VOTE, VOTE! This great privilege of democracy is too often left unused. Persistent expressions of concern, wrath, or anguish from voters carry enormous weight in the

> *We live on a planet that is terminally ill . . . . The United States has lost its direction and its soul. Use your democracy to save your world.*
>
> Helen Caldicott, M.D., 1986
> Former President, Physicians
> for Social Responsibility

halls of Congress. Candidates should be nominated and elected on the basis of their policies for planethood. Ideologues of narrow vision who believe a better world can be built by the arrogant brandishing of military might should be voted out of office. Young people who today may not be motivated to vote must learn that they *can* make a difference, and that there is a future for them.

Many political leaders believe that refusal to make concessions is evidence of strong character which will endear them to their constituents and coerce their opponents. They mistake stubbornness for strength and fail to perceive the needs of the nuclear age. They mislead rather than lead the people they hope to protect. If those in high office are unwilling or unable to demonstrate the flexibility required to protect the future of humankind, every peaceful effort should be made to replace them.

Many peace organizations keep track of the voting records of all members of Congress. (See Appendix 1.) Their reports will show which members are voting for billions of taxpayers' dollars for increased killing capacity instead of for measures which support peaceful objectives. We as informed citizens must oppose everyone who slows down our progress toward a more tranquil future. Every action that moves humankind toward the desired goal must be supported and encouraged. No political leader can ignore the sustained cry of the people.

> *Details are not crucial; the important point is to find a plan for peace that would be both effective and generally acceptable. If a sufficient effort is made, the effective wisdom of mankind can find the right combination.*
>
> Professor Louis Sohn, 1982
> Coauthor, *World Peace Through World Law*

FORWARD TO PLANETHOOD

A handful of politicians, military leaders, and industrialists with narrow vision cannot be allowed to determine the fate of humankind. The earth may have begun with a big bang, but no one vested a few mortals with the right to decide that it should end the same way.

All of the essential ingredients for a peaceful world are interrelated and linked. Progress in attaining one component stimulates acceptance of other components; likewise, failure to advance in one area impedes progress elsewhere. Like the fingers of the hand, all the parts must move together in a firm and coordinated way.

> *Let us resolve to bring our heroic energy together to build a new world that integrates the wisdom of the heart with the wisdom of the mind.*
> Ken and Penny Keyes
> *Gathering Power Through Insight and Love*

Just as no private citizen would surrender weapons if there were an armed and belligerent neighbor in the area where laws, courts, and police were nonexistent, so too, no nation can be expected to destroy all of its military might as long as there are no other means available for maintaining security, freedom, justice, and peace. If we wish to stop the stockpiling of nuclear death, we must establish a world system where international law, courts, and enforcement are a reality. *It is much too dangerous to remain trapped in the mortal embrace of our nuclear balance of terror.*

Let's use whatever influence we have, and whatever strength we can muster, to make sure that current international problems are dealt with in ways that support the ultimate goal of world peace through world law. By doing our deeds for planethood, we can put the necessary parts in place so that the house of peace will rest on a firmer foundation than it does today.

When he addressed the United Nations in 1984, President Reagan said:

> For the sake of a peaceful world, a world where human dignity and freedom is respected and enshrined, let us approach each other with tenfold trust and thousandfold affection. A new future awaits us. The time is here, the moment is now.

On April 10, 1987, Mikhail Gorbachev publicly accepted the idea of nuclear disarmament "under strict control" and verification. He called for a new social revolution by "the development of all forms of representative and direct democracy . . . ." His book *Perestroika: New Thinking for Our Country and the World* (Harper and Row, 1987) concluded:

> We want people of every country to enjoy prosperity, welfare and happiness. The road to this lies through proceeding to a nuclear-free non-violent world. We have embarked on this road, and call on other countries and nations to follow suit.

Today you have the greatest opportunity you will ever have to make your life deeply count to save yourself, your family, and the human species. It is an opportunity to stand tall with the good feeling that you are engaged in the *noblest purpose* that has ever motivated any human being in the history of the world. You can rededicate your life to our freedom and to our future: to freedom from war and a future of humanity on earth.

Never have you been challenged so profoundly. Never have you been given such a great opportunity to use all that is noble and good within you. Never have you been given such a global opportunity to secure our long-term human future. Never have the stakes been so high in the game of life. Never have your efforts been more needed than at the present moment in world history. Never has the world been so dependent upon you.

> For I dipt into the future,
>   far as human eye could see,
> Saw the Vision of the world,
>   and all the wonder that would be;
> . . . .
> Till the war-drum throbb'd no longer,
>   and the battle-flags were furl'd
> In the Parliament of man,
>   the Federation of the world.
>   Alfred Lord Tennyson
>   "Locksley Hall," 1842

Power lies with YOU. *We mean you.* After all the promises that have been made to you, all the beautiful words said by politicians, all the declarations that have been universally accepted, and with all of the great promise of the 21st Century, it is time for you to assert your ultimate human right to live in a peaceful world free from the threat of death by nuclear war.

Let your planethood voice be heard—loud and clear throughout the world! You will become a Peace Patriot bringing in a new era of world harmony. Through your dedication to this noble cause, you can award yourself with a personal peace prize for having done your best for humankind.

Then we can all enjoy the greatest prize:

Peace on Earth!
Goodwill toward all!

Eight Steps to
PLANETHOOD

1. Insist on Your Ultimate Human Right
2. Understand What Needs to Be Done
3. Become a Peace Patriot
4. Recognize Our Great Progress
5. Discover How to Make the U.N. Effective for the Nuclear Age
6. Tell Your Friends and Neighbors
7. Do Your Daily Deed for Peace
8. Give Yourself a Peace Prize!

Begin Today!

Acknowledgments

We wish to acknowledge the unacknowledged contributions to this book that have been made by so many people. In a book written for a broad audience, we felt it would be inappropriate to footnote every phrase or idea as in scholarly presentations. Our deep thanks and appreciation go out to all who have contributed to the mainstream of ideas that helps us understand what each of us must do to give our children a life on this planet.

Professor Robert H. Manley of Seton Hall University; Robert Muller, with 38 years of service in the U.N.; and Rear Admiral Gene R. LaRocque, (U.S. Navy Ret.), Director, Center for Defense Information kindly consented to read the manuscript for accuracy. We especially appreciate the suggestions of Walter Hoffman, Executive Director of the World Federalist Association.

Eric Cox of the Campaign for U.N. Reform deserves recognition for having inspired the preparation of this book. Gertrude Ferencz has been a constant source of comfort, encouragement, and enlightenment. Martin Segal of Florida and Donald Ferencz also gave many thoughtful suggestions.

Penny Keyes worked day and night editing and proofreading this book. Ann Hauser generously contributed her artistic talents and brilliantly did the complicated typesetting. Lynne Tuft donated all the circular drawings used throughout the book. Patrice Ziegenfuss and Carolyn Talbott of Love Line Books assisted in preparing this book for publication. Rik Burkhart suggested the title *PlanetHood*.

We especially thank *Reader's Digest* and Mrs. Emery Reves for permission to reprint material from *The Anatomy of Peace* by Emery Reves. Appreciation is given to the following authors and publishers for short quotations in this book: to Harper and Row from *Union Now* by Clarence Streit and *The World Must Be Governed* by Vernon Nash; to *Look* magazine for the excerpt from the article "Why Waste Time Discussing Disarmament?" by Emery Reves; to Richard Hudson of the Center for War/Peace Studies for material on the Binding Triad; to the Campaign for U.N. Reform for "A 14-Point Program for Reforming the United Nations"; to Tom Hudgens for permission to quote from *Let's Abolish War*; to the American Movement for World Government for "Essentials of a World Federal Government"; to Little, Brown and Company for excerpts from *Miracle at Philadelphia* by Catherine Drinker Bowen and excerpts from *Peace or Anarchy* by Cord Meyer; and to Viking Penguin for quotations by Carl Van Doren from *The Great Rehearsal: The Story of Making and Ratifying the Constitution of the United States*. To these and other sources, we offer our deepest appreciation.

Benjamin B. Ferencz
New Rochelle, New York

Ken Keyes, Jr.
Coos Bay, Oregon

APPENDIX 1

Expanding Your Personal Power

To rescue yourself and all of humanity, it is important that you know what you are talking about. Simply being for peace and against war is not enough. To add to your insurance for living into the 21st Century, you may wish to invest in the books below—and then absorb them as though your life depended on it—for it really does. You can also expand your personal power by writing for the literature of the organizations listed in this appendix.

TO INCREASE YOUR UNDERSTANDING

Your local library offers many resources on the U.N. and on America's political bicentennial. Here are some books that can give you a lot of information quite rapidly:

A Common Sense Guide to World Peace by Benjamin B. Ferencz. New York: Oceana Publications, 1985. $15 hardcover, $5 paperback. This book with less than 100 pages is in three parts: what *has* been done; what *should* be done; what *can* be done. It is packed with information.

*The Great Rehearsal: The Story of Making and Ratifying the Constitution of the United State*s by Carl Van Doren. New York: Viking Penguin, Inc., 1987. $6.95 in the paperback Penguin edition. This enjoyable book tunes you into the political wisdom, the attitudes of compromise, and the craftsmanship with which the founding fathers of the United States put the U.S.

Constitution together. It gives you a front row preview of what you need to do to support revising and reforming the Charter of the United Nations. That's why it's called *The Great Rehearsal*.

World Federalist Bicentennial Reader compiled by Barbara M. Walker. Washington, D.C.: World Federalist Association. 1987. $5.00. This is a gold mine for serious students and teachers who wish to deepen their understanding of the ingredients that go into building a successful constitution. It may be ordered directly from the World Federalist Association, 418 Seventh Street, S.E., Washington, D.C. 20003.

FOR ADVANCED STUDY

Here's a list of books by Benjamin B. Ferencz that spell out in detail the things we must do to establish a new international system to insure world peace:

Enforcing International Law—A Way to World Peace: A Documentary History and Analysis by Benjamin B. Ferencz. 2 volumes. New York: Oceana Publications, Inc., 1983.

Defining International Aggression—The Search for World Peace: A Documentary History and Analysis by Benjamin B. Ferencz. 2 volumes. New York: Oceana Publications, Inc., 1975.

An International Criminal Court—A Step Toward World Peace: A Documentary History and Analysis by Benjamin B. Ferencz. 2 volumes. New York: Oceana Publications, Inc., 1980.

NETWORKING WITH ORGANIZATIONS

In addition to the above books, as a modern Peace Patriot you may wish to become a member of one or all of the following organizations that are devoted to the cause of replacing the law of force with the force of law. They don't require it, but we suggest that you send them \$2 to help cover postage and printing costs of the information they will send you. Both volunteer helpers and monetary contributions are urgently needed to do their noble work in time to save humanity:

WORLD FEDERALIST ASSOCIATION
418 Seventh Street, S.E.
Washington, D.C. 20003
Phone: (202) 546-3950
Toll Free: 1-800-HATE WAR

CAMPAIGN FOR U.N. REFORM
418 Seventh Street, S.E.
Washington, D.C. 20003
Phone: (202) 546-3956

CENTER FOR WAR/PEACE STUDIES
218 East 18th Street
New York, NY 10003
Phone: (212) 475-1077

PARLIAMENTARIANS GLOBAL ACTION
211 East 43rd Street, Suite 1604
New York, NY 10017
Phone: (212) 687-7755

AMERICAN MOVEMENT FOR WORLD GOVERNMENT
World Government Center
One World Trade Center, Suite 7967
New York, NY 10048
Phone: (212) 524-7706

WORLD ASSOCIATION FOR WORLD FEDERATION
Leliegracht 21, 1016 GR
Amsterdam, The Netherlands
Phone: (020) 227502

or

United Nations Office
777 United Nations Plaza
New York, NY 10017
Phone: (212) 599-1320

WORLD CITIZENS ASSEMBLY
2820 Van Ness Avenue
San Francisco, CA 94109
Phone: (415) 474-9773

WORLD CONSTITUTION AND PARLIAMENT ASSOCIATION
1480 Hoyt Street, Suite 31
Lakewood, CO 80215
Phone: (303) 233-3548

WORLD FEDERALISTS OF CANADA
46 Elgin Street, Suite #32
Ottawa, Ontario K1P 5K6
Phone: (613) 232-0647

UNITED NATIONS ASSOCIATION—U.S.A.
485 Fifth Avenue
New York, NY 10017-6104
Phone: (212) 697-3232

PROFESSIONALS' COALITION FOR NUCLEAR ARMS CONTROL
1616 P Street, N.W.
Washington, D.C. 20036
Phone: (202) 332-4823

EDUCATORS FOR SOCIAL RESPONSIBILITY
23 Garden Street
Cambridge, MA 02138
Phone: (617) 492-1764

GLOBAL EDUCATION ASSOCIATES
475 Riverside Drive
New York, NY 10115
Phone: (212) 870-3290

CAMPAIGN FOR WORLD GOVERNMENT
331 Park Avenue
Glencoe, IL 60022
Phone: (312) 835-1377

APPENDIX 2

Highlights of the United Nations

The United Nations was created to prevent war by providing Governments with means for regular contact, cooperation, and collective action. Though international conflicts have continued, over the last 40 years Governments have been able to agree on common positions in a surprising number of matters. In the process, the essential foundations for a peaceful world have been strengthened. The United Nations system has become the world's main source of international law, codifying and creating more of it in four decades than in all previous history. In the area of human rights, its work has been pioneering. The protection of human rights is acknowledged now to be a legitimate concern of the international community: global standards have been set and binding agreements negotiated for the observance of a wide range of basic rights.

The United Nations has eased the passage to freedom of millions of people in former colonial territories, and focused international attention and support for ancient societies transforming themselves with modern science and technology. It has led a worldwide cooperative effort to deal with such urgent problems as population growth and environmental hazards, the effects of which transcend all national borders. For millions caught unprotected in the tumultuous processes of change—poor children, political refugees, victims of disaster—the Organization has brought the healing touch of attention and care. The chronology below is by no means a comprehensive listing;

it merely indicates the vast scope of United Nations activities over the last four decades.

1945: On June 26 the Charter of the United Nations is signed in San Francisco. The Second World War has ended in Europe but continues in Asia; its end there coincides with the terrible dawn of the nuclear age. ● The U.N., created on October 24, is at the center of a system of specialized agencies, some newly founded, others created decades earlier.

1946: In January, the *General Assembly* meets for the first time, in London, and elects the members of the *Security Council*, the *Economic and Social Council*, and the *International Court of Justice*. ● The first resolution the Assembly adopts is on disarmament, on the peaceful use of nuclear energy. Over the next four decades, as the arms race spirals upward, the Organization keeps the problem high on the international agenda. ● Other major problems considered by the first Assembly: decolonization, racial discrimination in South Africa, and the growing violence between Arabs and Jews in Palestine. ● In October the Assembly meets in New York, picked as headquarters for the Organization. It establishes the *United Nations Children's Fund.* ● The *Trusteeship Council* is set up.

1947: The Assembly adopts a plan that would, at the end of the British Mandate in Palestine in 1948, partition it into an Arab State and a Jewish State with Jerusalem under U.N. administration. The Organization's involvement in the region continues unabated over the next four decades as it seeks peace with equity for all parties involved.

1948: The *Universal Declaration of Human Rights* is adopted without opposition in the Assembly, marking the first time in history that such a document is endorsed by the international community. ● The cold war is at its height and the Secretary-General reports that the U.N. is virtually the only place where East and West have regular contact. ● U.N. military observers are sent to the Middle East and South Asia. ● International statistical services are resumed after an interruption of almost a decade as the U.N. Secretariat begins to collect, analyze, and publish data from around the world.

1949: Consultations initiated at the U.N. lead to a resolution of the crisis over Western access to the divided city of Berlin. ● The Assembly creates an agency to look after the welfare of the hundreds of thousands of Palestinian refugees in the Middle East. ● The U.N. and the specialized agencies begin an *Expanded Program of Technical Assistance* to help economic and social development in poorer countries. ● Experts from more than 50 countries attend the *U.N. Scientific Conference on Conservation and Utilization of Resources.*

1950: The Security Council calls on Member States to help the southern part of Korea repel invasion from the north. (The Soviet Union is absent from the Council then, in protest against the exclusion of the People's Republic of China from the U.N.) ● At the initiative of the U.N., the *World Census Program* gets under way, aiming at a global head-count every decade: the first such assessment in history. ● The *U.N. Cartographic Office* is set up and coordinates with Governments involved in producing a map of the world on the millionth scale. ● The Economic and Social Council (ECOSOC) adopts the *Standard International Trade Classification,* the basis on which all statistics on world trade are now gathered.

1951: The Office of *U.N. High Commissioner for Refugees,* established by the General Assembly, takes over from the *International Refugee Organization.* The conference convened by the Assembly adopts a *Convention on Refugees,* spelling out their rights and international standards for their treatment. ● ECOSOC Regional Commission for Asia initiates studies of the Mekong River which lead to one of the largest river basin development projects attempted internationally.

1952: The General Assembly broadens its consideration of racial discrimination in South Africa to take up the entire question of *apartheid,* overriding South African objections that it is a matter entirely within its domestic jurisdiction. Over the next four decades, the Organization will be at the forefront of international efforts to fight a system of racism that the Assembly terms a "crime against humanity." ● The U.N. produces the first in a series of reports on the *World Social Situation*.

1953: Armistice in Korea results from initiatives made at the U.N. ● The *U.N. Opium Conference* in New York adopts international Protocol to control the production, trade, and use of the drug.

1954: The Secretary-General initiates quiet—and ultimately successful—negotiations for the release of American airmen held as prisoners of war in China. ● The *World Population Conference* convened by ECOSOC brings over 450 experts to Rome. They adopt no resolutions but it is evident that current knowledge of population trends is insufficient for decisions on economic and social policy. ● First signs of a thaw in the cold war appear as ECOSOC Regional Commission for Europe takes up trade relations between different economic systems. ● The U.N. High Commissioner for Refugees wins the first of two Nobel Peace Prizes; the second is awarded in 1981.

1955: The first *U.N. Congress on Prevention of Crime and Treatment of Offenders* sets minimum standards for the treatment of prisoners and for the training of personnel for correctional institutions. ● The first international conference on the *Peaceful Uses of Atomic Energy* convenes in Geneva and initiates a broad range of cooperation in the field.

1956: War in the Middle East over the Suez Canal is ended with the deployment of a U.N. peacekeeping force in the Sinai. ● A U.N. supervised plebiscite in British Togoland leads to the merging of that Territory with the Gold Coast to form the new State of Ghana.

1957: In the wake of Sputnik, the General Assembly takes up the peaceful uses of outer space. In the following years, it elaborates a new body of law to cover the exploration and use of outer space, including the Moon and other celestial bodies. ● The *International Atomic Energy Agency*, created by the General Assembly, begins work with headquarters in Vienna.

1958: The *U.N. Observer Group* helps defuse a Lebanon

160

crisis. ● The *Inter-Governmental Maritime Consultative Organization* begins work as a U.N. specialized agency, setting safe standards for shipping. ● The first *U.N. Conference on the Law of the Sea* adopts four landmark Conventions. ● French Togoland becomes independent after a U.N.-supervised plebiscite.

1959: The General Assembly adopts *Declaration of the Rights of the Child*. ● A *Special Fund* established by the General Assembly works in tandem with the *Expanded Program of Technical Assistance* to help developing countries explore areas into which private and public capital can be attracted. ● A U.N.-supervised plebiscite in the British Cameroons results in a part of the Territory being incorporated into Nigeria and another into the Cameroons.

1960: With the entry into the U.N. of 17 newly independent Territories, 16 of them African, the General Assembly assumes a much more active role in the process of decolonization. It adopts a *Declaration on the Granting of Independence to Colonial Countries and Peoples*, saying colonialism is a denial of basic human rights and calling for its swift end. ● At the request of the newly independent State of Congo, the largest ever U.N. peacekeeping force takes the field in an effort to save that mineral-rich country from destabilization and preserve its territorial integrity.

1961: Acknowledging that economic and social development in the poorer countries is basic to the achievement of international peace and security, the General Assembly declares the 1960's a *U.N. Development Decade*. U.N. capacity to deal with development problems is vastly increased during the decade.

1962: The Secretary-General plays a key role in resolving U.S.-Soviet confrontation over the issue of nuclear missiles in Cuba. ● The U.N. takes over administration of Dutch West New Guinea before transferring power to Indonesia. ● The *U.N. Observer Mission* aids peace efforts in Yemen.

1963: The U.N. and the Food and Agriculture Organization (FAO) set up the *World Food Program* to provide food and other commodity aid to needy countries, drawing on surpluses in donor countries. ● The Security Council calls for voluntary arms embargo against South Africa.

1964: *U.N. Conference on Trade and Development* declares trade a "primary instrument of development," and calls for a permanent secretariat to focus on the web of problems involved. A U.N. peacekeeping force is sent to Cyprus to keep communal peace. It stays over the following years as talks under U.N. auspices seek a peaceful solution.

1965: The *U.N. Observer Mission* helps disengagement of forces after war between India and Pakistan. ● Technical assistance activities get a big boost with the merger of the *Expanded Program* (1949) and the *Special Fund* (1959) to form the *U.N. Development Program* as the major channel of funding for the specialized agencies in the U.N. system. UNDP assumes an important coordinating role and extends a network of "resident representatives" to help aid delivery around the world. ● UNICEF is awarded the Nobel Peace Prize.

1966: Two major Covenants on human rights are adopted, one covering *Civil and Political Rights* and the other *Economic, Social, and Cultural Rights.* The former has an "Optional Protocol" allowing individual complaints to be considered by an international *Human Rights Committee.* Together, the two binding instruments cover most of the rights included in the 1948 *Universal Declaration of Human Rights.* ● The Security Council, for the first time in U.N. history, imposes mandatory sanctions against Southern Rhodesia, where a racist white minority Government unilaterally declared independence from Britain in 1965. ● The Assembly ends South Africa's Mandate over the Territory of South West Africa, saying it has failed to fulfill its obligations.

1967: After war erupts again in the Middle East, the Security Council adopts Resolution 242 which calls for withdrawal of forces from occupied territories and recognizes the right of all States in the area to security. It becomes a widely accepted basis for a settlement of the Middle East problem.

• The General Assembly, meeting in special session, sets up a U.N. Council to administer South West Africa.

1968: On the 20th anniversary of the Universal Declaration, an *International Conference on Human Rights* is convened by the General Assembly in Teheran. The first worldwide governmental meeting on the whole range of human rights, it reaffirms the Declaration, and chalks out further priorities for U.N. action.

1969: *The Convention on Elimination of All Forms of Racial Discrimination,* adopted by the General Assembly in 1965, comes into force. Parties to the Convention condemn racial discrimination and *apartheid* and undertake to adopt policies for their elimination without delay.

1970: An *International Development Strategy* is adopted for the *Second Development Decade* declared by the General Assembly. Targets are set for different groups of countries and for increases in aid and industrial and agricultural production. • The General Assembly adopts the first internationally agreed set of principles on the vast area of seabed and ocean floor beyond national jurisdiction. The first principle declares the area to be the "common heritage" of humanity.

1971: The International Court of Justice, in an advisory opinion requested by the Security Council, declares the continued presence of South Africa in Namibia "illegal." • The Assembly restores "lawful rights" of the People's Republic of China in the U.N. • Bahrain becomes independent after the U.N. helps resolve an Iran-United Kingdom dispute on the status of territory. • Massive U.N. relief effort aids victims of conflict in East Pakistan (later Bangladesh).

1972: The U.N. *Environment Conference* meets in Stockholm, and adopts a historic declaration on the need for new principles to govern human activities in order to safeguard the natural world. The Assembly sets up a *U.N. Environment Program* to catalyze action in that regard. • The *U.N. Disaster Relief Organization,* created by the General Assembly to keep tabs on and coordinate international aid in emergencies, becomes operational.

1973: Another war in the Middle East ends with new U.N. peacekeeping forces in the Sinai and the Golan Heights. ● The Assembly bases *U.N. University* in Tokyo to coordinate and marshal efforts by the world's intellectual communities to deal with global problems.

1974: After a breakdown of the world monetary system of fixed currency exchange values, amidst energy and food crises, the Assembly calls for a *New International Economic Order* as a stable basis for interdependent world economy. ● World conferences on population and food assess the current situation and underline need for a global change. ● Inter-communal talks in Cyprus are convoked by the Secretary-General.

1975: *World Conference of the International Women's Year* convenes in Mexico City and adopts a *Declaration on Equality of Women and Their Contribution to Development and Peace.* A Plan of Action for the next ten years provides for world conferences to review progress at the mid-point and end of the *U.N. Decade for Women.*

1976: To deal with perennial problems of low and erratic prices of raw materials in world trade (on which most developing countries depend), the *U.N. Conference on Trade and Development* adopts the *Integrated Program* involving a new Fund to finance buffer stocks and a range of individual commodity agreements. ● A conference on human habitat plans action.

1977: The Security Council makes the arms embargo against South Africa mandatory. ● A billion dollar *International Fund for Agricultural Development,* a new U.N. specialized agency, begins to finance food production in developing countries.

1978: The General Assembly convenes in special session, for the first time on the topic of disarmament, and succeeds in drawing up a framework for future action and a set of priorities. ● The Security Council adopts a plan put forward by five Western countries for the independence of Namibia. ● A U.N. peacekeeping force is sent to Lebanon.

1979: The General Assembly adopts a *Convention on the Elimination of Discrimination Against Women,* covering political, economic, social, cultural, and civil rights.

1980: As the result of an international campaign coordinated by the *World Health Organization,* smallpox is totally eradicated from the world. The cost of the program to WHO is about what the world spends on arms in three hours.

1981: The General Assembly adopts *Declaration on Elimination of All Forms of Intolerance and Discrimination Based on Religion or Belief.* ● The *Conference on New and Renewable Sources of Energy* maps action.

1982: After nine years of complex and painstaking work, the Conference convened by the Assembly adopts what could be the most significant legal instrument of the century, the wide-ranging *Convention on the Law of the Sea.* ● Secretary-General Pérez de Cuéllar's first annual report to the Assembly warns of a trend toward world anarchy and urges rededication to Charter principles on the use of the U.N. as an instrument for peace and rational change.

1983: The Secretary-General visits southern Africa to consult on how the Security Council plan for independence of Namibia can be implemented. Virtually all outstanding issues are resolved, but South Africa's insistence on the withdrawal of Cuban troops from neighboring Angola before implementation of the plan makes its initiation impossible.

1984: After seven years of work in the *Commission on Human Rights,* the General Assembly adopts a *Convention Against Torture,* hailed as a major step toward creating a more humane world. ● The Assembly also adopts a Declaration on the critical economic situation and famine in Africa.

1985: The *Office for Emergency Operations,* created by the Secretary-General, spearheads massive famine relief effort in Africa.

1986: The U.N. mobilizes a massive international aid program for drought-stricken African countries. ● In the aftermath of the Chernobyl accident, the *International Atomic Energy*

Agency of the U.N. adopts two international conventions on early notification of atomic accidents and emergency mutual assistance. ● The Secretary-General of the U.N. successfully mediates the problem between New Zealand and France about the sinking of the Greenpeace boat.

1987: The *U.N. Environment Program* obtains international agreement and signature of a world convention on the protection of the ozonosphere. ● The U.N. convenes the first world conference on drug abuse and control of illicit traffic of drugs.

Taken from *For a Better World* published by
the United Nations, United Nations Plaza,
New York, N.Y. 10017

APPENDIX 3
The Anatomy of Peace
by Emery Reves

*In 1945, a widely heralded book called for a demo-
cratic reorganization of human society to ensure individual liberties and peaceful human relationships. It
did not call for giving up something; it called for
creating new legal institutions we had never had and
which were imperatively needed. The author, Emery
Reves, traced our history to show that in the modern
age, the completely independent sovereign nation-state
was obsolete. If the unregulated anarchy in international affairs was to be ended, law and order would
have to be extended into the international field. Local
affairs could be handled by local governments, and
national affairs by national governments, but the regulation of international affairs and the maintenance of
peace would require a form of world government.*

*A condensation of the Reves book published by
Harper and Brothers in 1945 appeared in the* Reader's
Digest. *Since it is still so perceptive and appropriate
today, part two is reprinted here with the permission of
Mrs. Emery Reves and the* Reader's Digest.

20TH CENTURY FEUDALISM

CONDITIONS prevailing today in human society show striking
parallels with conditions in the era between the tenth and 13th
centuries, when feudalism flourished.

When the centralized rule of the known Western World collapsed with the fall of the Roman Empire, the lives and property of the people were stripped of protection against either internal marauders or foreign invaders. From this chaotic stage of Western evolution emerged feudalism, a political system which was brought into being by the desire of the masses for security. The landless freeman and the small landowner went to the most powerful lord in the neighborhood and asked for shelter and support, offering their services in exchange.

The subjects submitted themselves and their lands—if they had any—to the baron, and received from him food and shelter in peacetime and equipment in war, for which they tilled the soil, paid taxes and fought battles. Sovereign power was, for all practical purposes, vested in the individual barons.

The relations between the lords and their subjects were established by custom and regulated by law, but the relationships between the neighboring lords were unregulated except by family ties, friendships, and agreements between them. Naturally, jealousies and rivalries soon flared up among the individual lords who more and more frequently called upon their subjects to fight the subjects of a neighboring lord.

As intercommunications developed and as populations grew, the conflicts between these units increased in frequency and violence. Each feudal lord looked upon the power and influence of his neighbors with fear and suspicion. There was no way to obtain security against attack other than to defeat one's neighbor, conquer his lands, incorporate his subjects, thereby widening one's own sphere of influence.

This evolution culminated in complete chaos with almost permanent fights. It took a long time for the subjects to realize that the contracts they had entered into with the feudal barons to obtain security and protection had brought them instead permanent wars, insecurity, misery and death.

Finally, however, they found that their salvation could be achieved only by establishing a government which would stand above the quarreling and warring barons. To achieve this it was necessary to destroy the power of the feudal landlords and to establish direct relations between the subjects and the central government. So the people rallied around the kings, who became strong enough to impose a superior legal order. The feudal system, which had dominated the world for five long centuries, disintegrated as soon as better means of intercommunication and the growth of common ideas made wider government possible.

What does this long and painful history of medieval society have to do with our problem in the 20th century? The human race has continually struggled for the best forms and methods to achieve a social order within which man can have both freedom and security. The historical evolution of society proves that these human ideals are best achieved if the individual is in direct relationship with a supreme, central, universal source of law. Twice in the history of Western civilization this truth has found institutional expression: in the monotheistic religions and in democracy.

The fundamental doctrine of the Jewish, Christian and Mohammedan religions is monotheism, the oneness of God— the Supreme Lawgiver—the basic belief that before God every man is equal. This doctrine is the rock upon which modern Western civilization is built. The establishment of a single universal God as the Supreme Being and unique source of authority over mankind revealed for the first time the only lawmaking system upon which peaceful human society can be erected.

At the time this thesis of society was proclaimed, conditions were far too primitive to permit its application as a political doctrine. For a long time, therefore, the concept of equality under universal law flourished only as a religious faith. In the 18th century, however, conditions at last induced the fathers of modern democracy to open a crusade to destroy the sovereignty of the many kings and rulers who oppressed and enslaved the people. The crusade led to the proclamation of the basic principle that sovereignty resides in the community, in the people.

This principle, the very foundation of democracy, represents the political corollary of monotheism. The thesis is that the will of the community is the one source of law, and that under that law every man is to be regarded as equal. It is one of the great tragedies of history that the recognition and proclamation of this principle came a century too early.

When it became the dominating doctrine, the universality of law was not yet technically possible. The world was still too big, it could not yet be centrally controlled, it was still an exclusively agricultural planet with economic conditions scarcely different from those of antiquity. So a substitute presented itself which permitted the new doctrine of democratic sovereignty to find immediate practical expression.

This substitute was the nation. In the 18th century, society could not possibly be organized universally. Consequently, democracy could not be organized according to its fundamentally universal principles. It had to be organized nationally.

For a long time the problem seemed to have been satisfactorily solved and citizens and subjects of the modern democratic nation-states enjoyed a hitherto unknown degree of freedom, security and welfare.

But soon, under the tremendous increase of intercommunication, the various sovereign national units were brought into close contact with each other. Just as in the medieval age, these contacts between sovereign units created frictions and conflicts.

Today, far from enjoying freedom, far from obtaining the expected security and protection from their nation-states, the citizens are constantly exposed to oppression and violence. The multiplicity of the conflicting sovereign units in our society destroys every vestige of the freedom, protection and security originally granted by nation-states.

In the middle of the 20th century, we are living in an era of absolute political feudalism in which the nation-states have replaced the barons. The arbitrary and artificial segregation of human society compels nation-states to act in exactly the same way toward their subjects and their neighbors as did the feudal lords.

In the nation-state system, we are unable to participate in the creation of law in any part of human society beyond our own country. It is, therefore, a self-delusion to say that Americans, Englishmen or Frenchmen are "free people." They can be attacked by other nations and forced into war at any time. They are living in a state of fear and insecurity just as great as under tyrants who interfered with their liberties at will.

This system of nation-feudalism has plunged the world into unprecedented barbarism, and destroyed almost all individual rights and human liberties secured with so much toil and blood by our forefathers.

There is not the slightest hope that we can change the course into which we are rapidly being driven by the conflicting nation-states so long as we recognize them as the supreme and final expression of the sovereignty of the people. At ever increasing speed we shall be hurled toward greater insecurity, greater destruction, greater hatred, greater barbarism, until we resolve to destroy the political system of nation-feudalism and establish a social order based on the sovereignty of the community, as conceived by the founders of democracy and as it applies to the realities of today.

THE ONE REAL CAUSE OF WAR

IT IS commonly taken for granted that war has innumerable causes and that to try to abolish all of them would be a hopeless task.

We must refuse to accept such an apparently true but basically deceptive statement, if we would avoid becoming the helpless victims of superstition.

Superficially, it looks as though wars have been waged for a great variety of reasons. Among primitive people, families, clans and tribes fought, enslaved and exterminated each other for food, shelter, women, hunting grounds. Later, at a higher level of civilization, we see larger settlements and towns fighting and warring with each other—Nineveh, Babylon, Troy, Athens,

Sparta, Rome and Carthage. Following the collapse of the feudal system, the field of conflict again shifted, and wars were fought by great commercial centers, Venice, Florence, Hamburg, Danzig and other city units. Then another series of wars were waged by absolute monarchs in the interest of their dynasties, and still another series by organized religions. And finally, the creation of modern nation-states brought about a series of gigantic conflicts between whole conscripted nations.

Looking back over history, war appears a hundred-headed hydra. As soon as the peacemakers chop off one head, new ones immediately appear on the monster. Yet, if we analyze what seem to be the manifold causes of past wars, we observe a thread of continuity. The real cause of all wars has always been the same.

> Wars between groups of men forming social units always take place when these units—tribes, dynasties, churches, cities, nations—exercise unrestricted sovereign power.

> Wars between these social units cease the moment sovereign power is transferred from them to a larger or higher unit.

The reasons alleged by history to have brought about these conflicts are irrelevant, as they continued to exist long after the wars had ceased. Cities and provinces continue to compete with each other. Religious convictions are as different today as they were during the religious wars.

Once the fundamental cause of wars—of all wars—is realized, the futility and childishness of passionate debates about armament and disarmament must be apparent.

If human society were organized so that relations between units in contact were regulated by democratically controlled legal institutions, then modern science could devise the most devastating weapons, and there would be no war. But if we allow sovereign rights to reside in the separate units without regulating their relations by law, then we can prohibit every weapon, even a penknife, and people will beat out each other's brains with clubs.

It is tragic to witness the utter blindness and ignorance of our governments and political leaders in regard to this all-important and vital problem.

After 1919, the peacemakers were obsessed by the idea that armaments lead to wars, that a *sine qua non* for world peace is the general limitation and reduction of armaments. Disarmament completely dominated international thought for 15 years. Tremendous amounts of propaganda were poured into the public ear to the effect that no nation should build battleships bigger than 35,000 tons, that the caliber of guns should be reduced, submarine and gas warfare prohibited, and so forth.

Now our leaders are preaching the exact opposite. We are told today that only powerful armaments can maintain peace, that the democratic nations must maintain omnipotent navies, air forces and mechanized armies, that we must control strategic bases spread around the globe.

This idea, the idea of maintaining peace by armaments, is just as complete a fallacy as the idea of maintaining peace through disarmament. Arms have as much to do with peace as frogs with the weather. Conscription and large armies are just as incapable of maintaining peace as no conscription and disarmament.

The problem of peace is a social and political problem, not a technical one.

WHAT SOVEREIGNTY REALLY MEANS

THE fundamental problem of peace is the problem of sovereignty. The welfare, the happiness, the very existence of a miner in Pennsylvania, Wales, Lorraine or the Don Basin, a farmer in the Ukraine, the Argentine, the American Midwest or the Chinese rice fields, depends upon the correct interpretation of sovereignty. This is not a theoretical debate but a question more vital than wages, prices and taxes, because the solution of all the everyday problems . . . depends upon the solution of the central problem of war.

The very fact that today there is so much talk of sovereignty—a word hardly mentioned in political discussions a decade or two ago—proves the existence of a sore spot in the body politic. It leaves no doubt that something is wrong with sovereignty, that the present interpretation of this notion is passing through a crisis and that clarification is necessary.

What does "sovereignty" mean?

At a very early stage of human society, it was discovered that before we could live together, in a family, in a tribe, it was necessary to impose certain restraints upon our natural impulses, to forbid certain things we like to do, and to compel us to do certain things we do not like to do.

Human nature is such that man does not accept rules unless they are imposed upon him by constituted authority. The first absolute authority was God.

So it was necessary to make people believe that the required rules and regulations were the express commands of God. They were proclaimed with all the magic at their command by priests, who had direct access to God and who knew how to proclaim His will, amid so much thunder and lightning that the people were frightened into accepting them.

Here we have the first sovereign authority—the first source of law—a supernatural symbol. Monarchs, emperors and kings, in order to maintain their authority and lawmaking power, to make people recognize them as the supreme source of law, linked themselves as closely as possible with religion and proclaimed that they derived the power from God.

Between the Renaissance and the 18th century, a revolutionary social ideal took shape—the principle that no individual, no family, no dynasty, could any longer be regarded as sovereign, that the sovereign lawgiving authority was the people. This revolutionary principle led to the establishment of the American and French republics, and to the "king reigns but does not rule" parliamentary system in England and many other countries.

THE IDEAL of national sovereignty, at its inception, was a great forward step and an incentive to human progress. The American Declaration of Independence, the French Revolution, following on the development of representative institutions in England, were an enormous encouragement to other peoples to fight for their own sovereignty and independence. The climax of this evolution was reached in the peace treaties of 1919, when more nations than ever before became completely sovereign and independent. Twenty years later all those proud national sovereignties lay trampled in the dust and today more people than ever before in modern history are enslaved and plunged into misery.

Why did this happen?

It happened because the political system established in 1919, an apotheosis of 18th-century ideals, was an anachronism, and in total contradiction to things as they are in the 20th century. The great ideals of national sovereignty, independence, nationality as the basis of states were wonderful achievements in the 18th century, in a world which was so vast before the Industrial Revolution had begun.

Our present conception of national sovereignty shows how an ideal, once realized, can be distorted in the span of a single century. The democratic conception of sovereignty meant the transfer of sovereign rights from one man, the king, to all men, the people. In the democratic sense, sovereignty resided in the community. We must try to visualize the world as it was in the 18th century. The Industrial Revolution had not even begun. The stagecoach was the fastest means of transportation. Under such conditions, the widest horizon of the forebears of democracy was—the nation. When they proclaimed the sovereignty of the nation, they meant the sovereignty of the community; they meant sovereignty to have the broadest possible basis.

As the world is organized today, sovereignty does *not* reside in the community, but is exercised in an absolute form by groups of individuals we call nations. This is in total contradiction to the original democratic conception of sovereignty. Today, sovereignty has far too narrow a basis; it no longer has the power it was meant to have. The word is the same. The conception it expresses is the same. But the surroundings have changed. The conditions of the world have changed.

The seeds of the 20th-century crisis began to germinate almost immediately after the establishment of the modern democratic nation-states. Quite independently something happened which was destined to become an equally strong movement and an equally powerful factor of human progress. That something was: Industrialism.

These two dominating currents of our age, nationalism and industrialism, are in constant and inevitable conflict with each other.

Industrialism tends to embrace the whole globe within its sphere of activity. Modern industrial mass production needs raw materials from all over the earth, and seeks markets in every corner of the world. It strives to achieve its purposes irrespective of political, geographic, religious, racial, linguistic or national barriers.

Nationalism, on the other hand, tends to divide this world into small independent groups.

For a century it was possible for these conflicting currents to flow side by side. In the new nation-state world, some compartments were large enough for industrialism to develop within them. But since the beginning of this century these two forces have clashed with titanic violence. It is this collision between our political life and our economic and technological life that is the cause of the 20th-century crisis with which we have been struggling since 1914, helpless as guinea pigs.

The meaning of this convulsion is clear. The political framework of our world with its . . . sovereign nation-states is an insurmountable obstacle to free industrial progress, individual liberty and social security.

If we refuse to understand this problem and dogmatically refuse to recognize that industrialism has made our political structure obsolete, then we cannot hope to create a political framework in this world within which industrialism, individual liberties and peaceful human relationship are possible.

THE FIRST STEP toward ending the present chaos is to overcome the tremendous emotional obstacle which prevents us from
realizing and admitting that the ideal of sovereign nation-states,
with all its great record of success during the 19th century, is
today the cause of all the immeasurable suffering and misery of
this world. We are living in complete anarchy, because in a small
world, interrelated in every other respect, there are ... [159] separate sources of law, ... [159] sovereignties.

The significant thing about the present crisis is that the
nation-states, even the most powerful, even the United States,
Great Britain and the Soviet Union, are no longer powerful
enough, no longer "sovereign" enough, to fulfill the purpose for
which they were created. They cannot prevent disasters like the
first and second world wars. They cannot protect their peoples
against the devastation of international war. And if the sovereignty of these great nations does not suffice to protect their
citizens, we need not even talk about the fictitious sovereignty of
Latvia or Rumania.

To put it plainly, the ideal of the nation-state is bankrupt.
The nation-state is impotent to prevent foreign aggression, it no
longer serves as the supreme institution capable of protecting its
people against the miseries and misfortunes that war brings. And
World War II has finally demonstrated that not a single nation,
even the most powerful, is economically self-sufficient.

The inescapable economic and technical realities of our age
make it imperative to re-examine the notion of sovereignty and
to create sovereign institutions based on the community, according to the original democratic conception. Sovereignty of the
people must stand *above* the nations so that under it each nation
may be equal, just as each individual is equal under the law in a
civilized state.

*The question is not one of "surrendering" national sover-
eignty. The problem does not involve giving up something we
already have. The problem is to create something we have never
had, but that we imperatively need.*

The creation of institutions with universal sovereign power is merely another phase of the same process in the development of human history—the extension of law and order into a field which heretofore has remained unregulated and in anarchy.

A few centuries ago, many cities held full sovereign rights. Later some portion of municipal sovereignty was transferred to provinces. Then to larger units and finally to the nation-states.

In the United States of America today, the problems of fire prevention, water supply, street cleaning and other similar matters are under municipal authority. The construction of roads, education, legislation regarding industrial and commercial enterprises, and endless other issues are under state sovereignty. And finally, problems affecting the United States Army, Navy, foreign policy, currency and other matters are under federal sovereignty.

As HUMAN progress continues, conditions require an ever-broader basis for sovereignty, for absolute power, to fulfill its purpose: the protection of the people.

New Yorkers are citizens of the city of New York, of the state of New York and of the United States of America. But they are also citizens of the world. Their lives, their security, their liberties are protected in a very wide field by the sovereign authority which resides in the people, who have delegated its exercise partly to the city of New York, partly to the state of New York and partly to the federal government of the United States of America.

If the state of New York enacted economic or social legislation that reacted harmfully on economic and labor conditions in Connecticut, and no higher sovereignty existed, such an act on the part of the sovereign state of New York could not be prevented by the sovereign state of Connecticut, except by war. But a higher sovereignty—the federal sovereignty—exists, and under it the state of New York and the state of Connecticut are equal. This higher sovereignty alone protects the people against such danger.

Democratic sovereignty of the people can be correctly expressed and effectively instituted only if local affairs are handled by local government, national affairs by national government, and international, world affairs, by international, world government. Only through such separation of sovereignties can we have a social order in which men may live in peace with each other, endowed with equal rights and equal obligations before law. Only in a world order based on such separation of sovereignties can individual freedom be real.

Sovereignty finds expression in institutions, but is not and never can be identical with any institution. To assume that sovereign rights must eternally reside in any specific institution—today the nation-state—to believe that the nation-state is *the* expression of sovereignty, is pure totalitarianism, the greatest foe of democracy.

The nation-states received their power from their peoples to carry out certain tasks. The moment established institutions fail to keep abreast of conditions in society and are unable to maintain peace, they become a source of great danger and must be reformed if violent social convulsions and wars are to be averted.

Necessary reform in this field does not require the abolition of nations and national boundaries. Within each nation-state, we still have state lines, county demarcations, city limits, boundaries of our home lots or of houses and apartments. Families have names of their own different from those of other families. We like, protect and defend our own families more than other families. We love our homes, pay allegiance to our own communities, our countrysides, our provinces.

But sovereign power is not vested in these units which divide us. Sovereign power is vested in the state, which unites us.

Should the people, who are the real source of sovereign power, conclude that in the international field they would be better protected by delegating part of their sovereignty to bodies other than the nation-states, then they would "surrender" nothing. Rather they would acquire something, namely law and order in a field where such law has never existed, and the protection of the lives and liberties of all peoples. What a gain it would be to transfer certain aspects of our sovereign rights from national legislative, judicial and executive bodies to universal bodies that are equally democratically elected and democratically controlled, in order to create, apply and execute law for the regulation of human relationships in the international field!

THE FALLACY OF PEACE TREATIES

IF AT any time since the Tower of Babel utter confusion has reigned in this world, it is today. Thousands of books and articles have been published about the all-important problem confronting us: how to establish a world order that will prevent global war. All the planners of lasting peace believe that theirs is the magic formula; that they can make something work which never has worked; that after the failure of thousands of peace treaties they can draft one that will prevent war.

Peace in a society means that relations among the members of the society are regulated by law, that there is a democratically controlled machinery of lawmaking, of jurisdiction, and that to carry out these laws the community has the right to use force, a right denied to the individual members of that community.

Peace is order based on law. There is no other imaginable definition. Any other conception of peace is sheer Utopia.

Each time a war is fought, it is followed by endless debate on the kind of treaty that will be made. Hundreds of suggestions are advanced, but no matter what kind of treaty is signed, the next war is inevitable.

Why?

Because the content of a treaty is irrelevant—the treaty idea itself is at fault.

We have had thousands and thousands of peace treaties in the history of mankind. None has survived more than a few years. None could prevent war, for the simple reason that human nature, which cannot be changed, is such that conflicts are inevitable as long as sovereign power resides in individual groups in society, and not in society itself.

If we seek peace between *x* sovereign units, based on treaty agreements, then peace is an impossibility and it is childish even to think of it. But if we conceive peace correctly, as order based on law, then peace is a practical proposition that can be realized just as well between the nation-states as it has been realized so often in the past between provinces, cities and other units when they have become part of a larger government.

Whether we are to have peace or continually recurring war depends on a very simple proposition.

It depends upon whether we want to base international relations on treaties, which are essentially static instruments, or on law, which is essentially a dynamic instrument.

Human society can never be mastered by static means, for it is a dynamic phenomenon par excellence. The essence of life is constant change, perpetual development. Up to now, peace between nations has always been a static conception. We have always tried to determine some sort of *status quo*, to seal it meticulously in a treaty, and to make any change in that *status quo* impossible except through war. This is a grotesque misconception of peace.

If we realize that peace is not a *status quo*, that it can never be a negative or a static conception, but that it is a *method*, a method of dealing with human affairs, then the problem of peace is clearly definable and perfectly solvable. Indeed, it has been solved many times in many fields, but always by the method of law, never by that of treaties. The two methods are qualitatively different and can never converge. We can never arrive at a legal order by means of treaties. If our goal is a society based on law, then it is imperative to start afresh.

A strange paradox lies embedded in the dogmatic minds of our statesmen and political thinkers. It is the traditional belief, inherited from the past and entirely dominating their outlook and actions, that there are two different ways of maintaining peace between men.

The one—universally recognized and applied *within* national, sovereign units, is—Law, Order, Government.

The other, so far used *between* sovereign national units, is—Policy, Diplomacy, Treaties.

This is a mental aberration, an utterly warped picture of the problem.

Peace can never be achieved by two such totally contradictory methods for the simple reason that peace is actually identical with one of those two methods.

Peace is law. It is order. It is government.

"Policy" and "diplomacy" not only may lead to war but cannot fail to do so because they are actually identical with war.

Several thousand years of social evolution have crystallized this axiom concerning any human society:

Peace among men can be achieved only by a legal order, by a sovereign source of law, a democratically controlled government with independent executive, legislative and judicial bodies. This is the only method that has proved capable of developing, of carrying out changes in human relations without violence. The other method, the method of diplomacy, the method tried and tried again to keep peace between sovereign units of any type and any size, the method dogmatically and stubbornly adhered to by our national governments, has invariably failed at all times, in all places and under all circumstances. To believe that we can maintain peace among men living in separated, sovereign national units by the method of diplomacy and policy, without government, without the creation of lawmaking institutions is a mere dream.

To TRY to prevent war by the use of policy is like trying to extinguish fire with a flame thrower.

Agreements and treaties between national governments of equal sovereignty can never last because such agreements and treaties are the products of mistrust and fear. Never of principles. Law is the only foundation upon which social life in modern society can exist. We cannot rely on men's promises not to murder, on their pledges not to steal, on their undertakings not to cheat. That is why we have to have laws and courts and police, with duties and functions clearly defined in advance.

In international relations we still talk about the "independence" of nations in absolute form, believing that a nation is independent only if it has absolute sovereignty to do whatever it wants, to sign treaties with other sovereign powers and to "decide" upon war and peace. We categorically reject any regulation of that national sovereignty on the ground that this would destroy national independence.

But such independence is illusory. For example, the United States of America, so unwilling to yield one iota of its national sovereignty, categorically refusing to grant the right to any world organization to interfere with the sovereign privilege of Congress to decide upon war and peace, was in 1941 forced into war by a decision made exclusively by the Imperial War Council in Tokyo. Is that independence?

The independence of a nation, like that of an individual, does not rest solely on its freedom of action, but equally on the degree to which the freedom of action of other nations may infringe upon its own independence. Only if we base international relations on law—just as we base on law the relations of individuals and groups within organized society—can we hope that the constant and inevitable evolution essential to life will be brought about by peaceful methods.

The dogma of "national sovereignty," which is supposed to overawe us, has no relevance in this connection. In either case—whether we stay on a treaty basis or set up a legal order—sovereignty is vested in the people. The difference is that in the treaty system sovereignty of the people is not exercised in sufficiently effective form because each sovereign nation-state has power over a limited area only, without any possibility of control over other sovereign nations seeking changes in the existing *status quo*; whereas in a world based on law, changes in international relations could for the first time be carried out without violence—by legally instituted procedure.

SUPER-STATE AND THE INDIVIDUAL

IN THIS ERA so prodigiously prolific of political slogans, another concept has been launched by the enemies of progress, a concept destined to become the object of passionate debate. This term is: super-state. It sounds terrifying. All men of healthy instincts are supposed to react in unison: We will have none of it! Any attempt to establish a legal order beyond the boundaries of the present nation-states is to be discredited and defeated by the rhetorical question: "Do you want to live in a super-state?"

But establishing a legal order over a wider area does not create a super-state. The criterion of a super-state is the degree to which it interferes with individual liberties. Mussolini's Italy was much more a "super-state" than the United States, though the latter is 25 times larger.

Our ideal is the democratic state. The state we want to live in is one which can guarantee us maximum individual liberty. But when, in this century, industrial progress began to undermine the old nation-state idea, each of the nation-states used artificial methods to reinforce its structure. A development started which, in the greater part of the world, led to the complete destruction of individual liberty.

In some countries, like Germany, Italy and Spain, this change was undertaken openly and purposely by suppressing individual liberty and proclaiming the principle that salvation lies in the all-powerful totalitarian nation-state endowed with the right to dispose of the very lives of its citizens. In other countries, like the United States, Great Britain and France, the development has been slow, gradual and against our will. We have continued to uphold democratic ideology but little by little we have given up more and more of our individual liberty to strengthen our respective nation-states.

It is wide of the mark to blame any particular political group or party. The trend was irresistible. Under the double threat of imminent and inescapable war, as pressure from outside, and economic crises and unemployment, as pressure from inside, it was and is imperative for each nation to strengthen its state by instituting or expanding military service, by accepting higher and higher taxation, by admitting more and more interference of the state in the everyday life of the individual.

It is a strange paradox that at any suggestion of a world-wide legal order which could guarantee mankind freedom from war for many generations to come, and consequently individual liberty, all the worshipers of the present nation-states snipe: "Super-state!"

For the reality is that the present nation-state has become a super-state. It is not a future nightmare or a proposal we can freely accept or reject. We are living within it now. And we shall become more and more subject to this all-powerful super-state if our supreme goal is to maintain the nation-state structure of the world. Under the constant threat of foreign war and under the boiling pressure of economic problems, insolvable on a national basis, we are forced to relinquish our liberties, one after the other. At the present stage of industrialism, the nation-states can maintain themselves in one way alone: by becoming super-states.

And there can be no freedom under such a system. Certainly, we cannot say that our individual freedom is guaranteed if every 20 years we have to stop production of consumer goods and waste all our energies and resources in the manufacture of the tools of war.

We cannot say that we have freedom of speech and the press when every 20 years conditions force censorship upon us.

We cannot say that private property is guaranteed if every 20 years gigantic public debts and inflation destroy our savings.

DEFENDERS OF national sovereignty will argue that all these restrictions and suppressions of individual liberty are emergency measures, necessitated by the exigencies of war, and cannot be regarded as normal.

Of course, they are emergency measures. But as the nation-state structure, far from being able to prevent war, is the only and ultimate cause of the recurrent international wars, and as the aftermath of each of these international wars is simultaneously the prelude to the next violent clash between the nations, 80 or 90 percent of our lives are spent in times of "emergency."

It is all the more important to recognize the primordial necessity of a universal, political and legal order because there is not the slightest possibility that we can solve any one of our economic or social problems in a world divided into scores of hermetically sealed national compartments.

It is pathetic to watch the great laboring masses of common men aspire to better conditions, higher wages, better education, more leisure, better housing, more medical care and social security. Yet under the certain threat of recurrent wars, all these social aspirations of the people are being indefinitely postponed. Even if in one country or another legislation to this effect is enacted, it will be crushed and buried by the next global war, like mountain huts by an avalanche.

Full employment within the compartmented political structure of sovereign nation-states is either a myth or fascism. Economic life can develop on a scale to provide work and goods for all only within a world order in which the permanent threat of war between sovereign nation-states is eliminated, and the incentive to strengthen the nation-states provided by the constant fear of being attacked and destroyed is replaced by the security that a legal order alone creates.

No matter how it hurts our most cherished dogmas, we have to realize that in our industrialized world, the greatest threat to individual liberty is the ever-growing power of the national super-state. The rights of the individual and human liberty, won at such a cost at the end of the 18th century through the overthrow of personal absolutism, are on the way to being completely lost to the new tyrant, the nation-state.

THE ASSERTION that the manifold differences existing in the human race prevent the creation of universal law and order is in flagrant contradiction to fact.

Poles and Russians, Hungarians and Rumanians, Serbs and Bulgars have disliked and distrusted each other and have been waging wars in Europe against each other for centuries. But these very same Poles and Russians, Hungarians and Rumanians, Serbs and Bulgars, once having left their countries and settled in the United States of America, cease fighting and are perfectly capable of living side by side without waging wars against each other.

Why is this? The change in one factor alone produced the miracle.

In Europe, sovereign power is vested in these nationalities and in their nation-states. In the United States, sovereign power resides not in any one of these nationalities but stands above them in the Union, under which individuals, irrespective of existing differences between them, are equal before the law.

The Germans and the French have distrusted and disliked each other and waged wars against each other for centuries. And yet, in Switzerland, situated between these hostile French and German nation-states, live about one million Frenchmen, as Gallic as any in the French Republic, and nearly three million Germans, as Germanic as any in the Reich, who have lived in peace for long centuries. The biological, racial, religious, cultural and mental differences are the same as exist between their recurrently warring kinsmen in the mother countries. Only one factor has changed.

The French people in France and the German people in Germany live in sovereign nation-states where sovereignty is vested respectively in the French nation and in the German nation. In Switzerland, sovereignty is vested not in the French nationality nor in the German nationality but in the union of both.

It seems, therefore, clear that friction, conflicts and wars between people are caused not by their national, racial, religious, social and cultural differences but by the *single fact* that these differences are galvanized in separate sovereignties which have no way to settle the conflicts resulting from their differences except through violent clashes.

Logical thinking and the experience of history agree that there *is* a way to prevent wars between the nations once and for all. But with equal clarity they also reveal that there is *one* way and one way alone to achieve this end: The integration of the scattered conflicting national sovereignties into one unified, higher sovereignty, capable of creating a legal order within which all peoples may enjoy equal security, equal obligations and equal rights under law.

This appendix is reprinted from *The Anatomy of Peace* by Emery Reves from *Reader's Digest* condensed version (part two of three parts) that appeared December, 1945. © 1945 by Emery Reves and published by Harper and Brothers, New York, NY.

APPENDIX 4

Circulate the Proclamation

Here's an action step you can take immediately to help secure your ultimate human right: You can circulate the proclamation on the next page. Make photocopies front and back and then sign up everyone you can. You may wish to set yourself the goal of filling one page every day.

Let's set our goals high. What we stand to gain is the greatest conceivable attainment: *the preservation of human life on earth.* Let's aim for millions of signatures gathered from people from all parts of the globe.

Speed is essential. If this proclamation proceeds in a chain letter fashion, we might have an enormous number of signatures within months. As you fill the pages, mail them to Mr. Javier Pérez de Cuéllar, Secretary-General, United Nations, New York, NY 10017-0000. Ask him to convey to the nations the strong desire of the people to live in a peaceful world system. You may wish to send the U.N. a donation to help their vital work for humanity.

You are making your life count in meeting the greatest crisis that has ever faced humanity!

PROCLAMATION!

My Ultimate Human Right

I have the right to live in a peaceful world free from the threat of death by nuclear war.

GOAL: MILLIONS OF SIGNATURES AS RAPIDLY AS POSSIBLE.

Name	Country

Please see other side.

Stand Up for Peace
and the Future of Humanity!

> *I like to believe that people in the long run are going to do more to promote peace than are governments. Indeed, I think that people want peace so much that one of these days governments had better get out of their way and let them have it.*
>
> **Dwight D. Eisenhower**
> Former U.S. President

> *We seek to strengthen the United Nations, to help solve its financial problems, to make it a more effective instrument for peace, to develop it into a genuine world security system . . . capable of resolving disputes on the basis of law, of insuring the security of the large and the small, and of creating conditions under which arms can finally be abolished . . . . This will require a new effort to achieve world law.*
>
> **John F. Kennedy**
> Former U.S. President

If you believe that the human species should not become extinct upon this planet, and you want the five billion people on earth to live in lasting peace, please add your name.

You can make a difference by copying this proclamation and circulating it as widely as possible. When sheets are full, mail them to: Mr. Javier Pérez de Cuéllar, Secretary-General, United Nations, New York, NY 10017-0000. Ask him to tell the nations how much the people of this world want lasting peace.

PROCLAMATION!

My Ultimate Human Right

I have the right to live in a peaceful world free from the threat of death by nuclear war.

GOAL: MILLIONS OF SIGNATURES AS RAPIDLY AS POSSIBLE.

Name	Country

Please see other side.

Stand Up for Peace
and the Future of Humanity!

> *I like to believe that people in the long run are going to do more to promote peace than are governments. Indeed, I think that people want peace so much that one of these days governments had better get out of their way and let them have it.*
>
> **Dwight D. Eisenhower**
> Former U.S. President

> *We seek to strengthen the United Nations, to help solve its financial problems, to make it a more effective instrument for peace, to develop it into a genuine world security system . . . capable of resolving disputes on the basis of law, of insuring the security of the large and the small, and of creating conditions under which arms can finally be abolished . . . . This will require a new effort to achieve world law.*
>
> **John F. Kennedy**
> Former U.S. President

If you believe that the human species should not become extinct upon this planet, and you want the five billion people on earth to live in lasting peace, please add your name.

You can make a difference by copying this proclamation and circulating it as widely as possible. When sheets are full, mail them to: Mr. Javier Pérez de Cuéllar, Secretary-General, United Nations, New York, NY 10017-0000. Ask him to tell the nations how much the people of this world want lasting peace.